CONTENTS

PREFACE

I would be remiss if I did not say a few words about the wonderful people who make up the world of quiltmaking. I have been refining the techniques described here for the last three years. My work started at what should have been the middle or end of the journey, not the beginning. As a result, I am sure I have unintentionally frustrated more than one student along the way.

The members of the Cottonwood Quilt Guild of Elkhorn, Nebraska; the Black Hills Quilt Retreat in New Castle, Wyoming; and the Capital Quilters of Bismarck, North Dakota, were willing subjects and taught me just how much I did not know. This book is a direct result of my experiences with them. It has been a long journey, but I found it intriguing and rewarding and I hope that you will too.

INTRODUCTION

I have always been fascinated by and enjoyed using 45-degree triangles. This book explores the exciting design possibilities of this versatile shape.

The designs presented here contain only two basic shapes, with an occasional square or right triangle used to complete a block. The first shape is the symmetrical 45-degree triangle, which has a 45-degree apex with two 67.5-degree angles at the base. This shape is often referred to as a Kaleidoscope triangle, and that is what I call it in this book. The second basic shape is an asymmetrical 45-22.5-112.5-degree triangle I call the "Wing." These triangles combine to form right triangles that are the building blocks of each quilt.

This book is aimed at the experienced quiltmaker who is ready for a challenge beyond the perpendicular. It is important that you have a good working relationship with your rotary cutter and that you can measure a square, sew accurate 1/4" seams, and recognize the straight grain of fabric.

I hope the piecing techniques and quilt designs in this book will present you with an enjoyable challenge. I love working with these shapes and want to pass the excitement along.

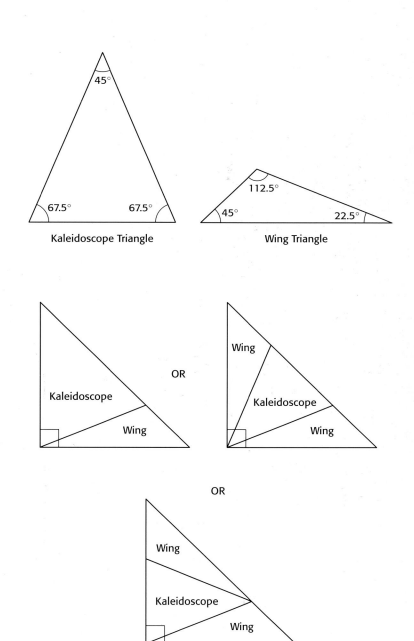

Kaleidoscope Triangle

Wing Triangle

HOW TO USE THIS BOOK

The quiltmaking instructions begin with the Simply Stellar Sampler. The Sampler is divided into three lessons, each covering one of the building blocks used in the projects in the book.

The rest of the book is divided into sections, each containing quilt projects based on a particular block. Each section builds on the previous one: the quilts based on Pieced Diamond blocks (Lesson Three) assume you know how to make Basic and Pinwheel blocks (Lessons One and Two).

I strongly recommend that you make the Simply Stellar Sampler. Going through each lesson in order and making all the blocks required for the Sampler will make you an expert at working with these triangles.

If you choose instead to dive right in and tackle another project, you must complete the lessons for the building blocks in your project. To do this, use scraps and cut and piece just a few of the shapes described in the relevant lesson. You don't need to cut all the strips and piece all the blocks required for the Sampler.

Customizing the Designs

Since quiltmaking is not a one-size-fits-all art form, I have provided work sheets—design grids—for the basic building blocks so that you can experiment with design and color. All you need is a copy machine; a pair of scissors; and some crayons, markers, or colored pencils.

Changing Quilt Sizes

Several of the quilt plans in this book are what I call "comfort size." This means the quilt is large enough to provide comfort and warmth for someone lounging on a sofa or chair but not large enough to use as a bedspread.

Most of the quilts were designed with expansion in mind. Some go from wall to queen size with a simple change of the Basic block size. Just remember to keep the block size in proportion to the quilt size. You wouldn't want to make a queen-size quilt top out of 4" stars (at least, I wouldn't), but the same design made with 8" or 12" stars would be wonderful to look at and saner to piece.

Another easy way to enlarge a quilt is to add borders. Several quilt plans in this book give optional border instructions. Just don't forget to adjust the fabric requirements when you change the size of the quilt, and remember that if you decide to enlarge the quilt after you've already bought fabric, a border is the perfect place to change fabrics.

Pieced borders made up of blocks that are the same dimensions as the building blocks are easiest. If you want to add a plain border before adding a pieced border, make the plain border's width equal to the size of the building blocks.

EQUIPMENT

Basic Supplies

You will need scissors, template plastic or other template material, a sewing machine, a square ruler (at least 6½" x 6½") with a 45-degree-angle line and ⅛" markings, a rotary cutter and mat, and a long quilter's ruler for cutting strips of fabric.

If you use templates, use a temporary spray adhesive to help the template stay put as you cut around it.

Mary Sue's Triangle Ruler

You can use handmade templates to make the blocks in this book (all the necessary ones are included), but you might consider replacing those templates with Mary Sue's Triangle Ruler, a tool specially designed for these blocks. You don't really need the ruler to make the Basic block, but it is extremely helpful for the more complex blocks. Please try the easy blocks and make your own determination, but I can guarantee that if you like this piecing system, you will love the ruler.

Mary Sue's Triangle Ruler is a quadrangle with 45-, 90-, and 112.5-degree corners.

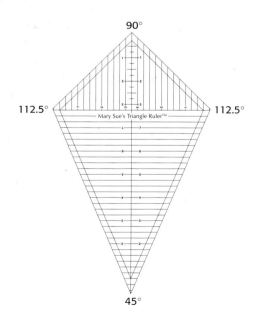

Two very important lines divide the ruler into sections: the center line runs from the 45-degree corner to the 90-degree corner, and the crossbar connects the two 112.5-degree angles. In addition, ¼" marks run parallel to these.

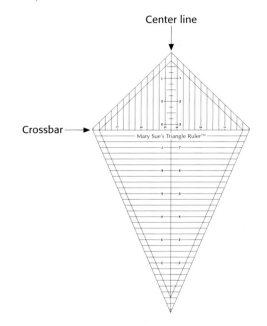

To cut Wing triangles, place the ruler so that the center line is horizontal. The center line marks the bottom of the triangle. The markings that extend from the crossbar to the 90-degree end of the ruler indicate the size of the Wing.

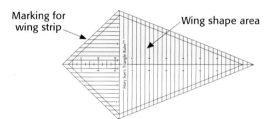

To cut Kaleidoscope triangles, place the ruler so that the crossbar is horizontal. The crossbar marks the short side of the Kaleidoscope. The markings that run parallel to the crossbar indicate the size of the piece.

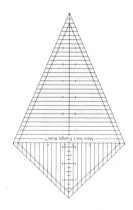

FABRIC SELECTION

When choosing fabric for a quilt, I usually take stock of what's on hand and choose something that appeals to me that day. I seldom have a color scheme in mind unless the quilt is for a specific person or use. Using the interesting fabric of the day as a guide, I then select coordinating colors.

If you have a definite color scheme in mind, which most people do, choose a multicolored print and pull colors from it. Don't, however, feel obliged to use the original print. Quite often the great fabric I start with ends up out of the quilt entirely, or on the back.

Be open to chance—some of my most dynamic color combinations have occurred because I did not clean up the cutting table.

Value

The value of a fabric—how light or dark it is—is more important than its color. The designs in this book require certain combinations of light, medium, and dark fabrics. I choose the best fabrics available that fit the value and color scheme.

Scale

Try to vary the scale of your prints, taking into account the size of the block. Make sure that you counter large-scale prints with small-scale motifs, and include "blender" fabrics that read as solid from a distance but are actually prints.

If I want the points in the block to look crisp and clear, I don't put two large-scale prints next to each other. For the designs in this book, batiks and mottled prints that give the illusion of light shining through them are wonderful—I like my quilts to appear backlit.

Pattern

I try to use a variety of patterns and colors. You will see small-scale traditional prints, batiks, plaids, floral prints, and mottled prints in my quilts.

As you look through this book, you'll notice that many quilts have unpieced solid or low-contrast border areas. These simple borders serve two purposes: they provide a place to show off hand or machine

quilting skills, and more important to the design, the plain areas give your eyes a rest. Pieced areas can be intense, so the viewer needs a chance to take in everything. Make a conscious effort to include at least one restful area within your quilt.

The fabrics you choose and the way you use them should be a reflection of you and only you. Whatever your taste in fabric, these designs will work, and your quilt will be as unique and as special as you are.

Fiber Content

As a rule, I use 100% cotton fabrics. However, I have been known to make exceptions. The exceptions usually occur in wall hangings or other small pieces not intended for constant use. These concessions are usually made in the name of a special color or an interesting texture.

Medium-weight cotton is the best fabric for the piecing techniques used in this book. Because some seam intersections will be bulky where multiple points converge, heavyweight fabrics might be difficult to use.

I preshrink my fabrics. Preshrinking gives me peace of mind and helps me keep up with the laundry.

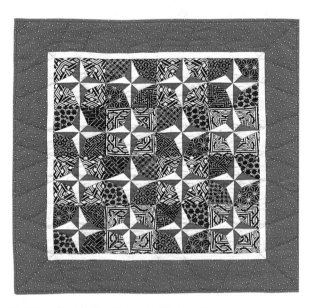

HURRAH by Phyllis Klein, 1998, Hay Springs, Nebraska, 28" x 36". This quilt uses the same Basic Star block as Twinkle, Twinkle Allover Star (page 31). The work sheet for this design appears on page 29. There are many options for the Allover Star setting. Try scraps on a muslin ground for a traditional look.

GENERAL TIPS

Cutting

For the quilts in this book, all the pieces are cut from strips. The fabric requirements are based on a usable width of 40", but your fabric may be slightly wider, so cut one strip at a time. You may need fewer strips than called for.

I don't cut selvages from my fabric before I cut strips, and the instructions in this book reflect that. If you prefer to trim selvages before cutting, ignore any mention of selvages and proceed with the cutting instructions.

I like to cut pieces just for the blocks I can put together that day. There is no reason to have a stack of pieces to store and keep track of until my next sewing opportunity. Some days I can cut and chain-piece many blocks; however, I often have more than one Monday in the week and need to switch to a block-by-block system. I always listen to my own rhythm. If I make the same silly mistake three times in a row, I leave the sewing room and do the dishes that are waiting for me.

Follow the cutting directions carefully. When the borders are longer than the width of the fabric, cut along the length of the fabric first, then cut crosswise strips from the remaining fabric for your triangles.

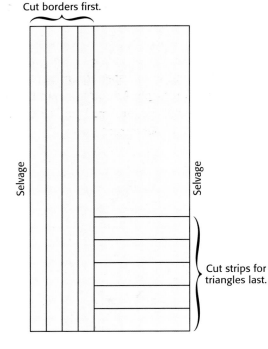

Cut borders first.

Selvage

Selvage

Cut strips for triangles last.

The cutting instructions and illustrations are for right-handed quilters. If you are left-handed, reverse the directions in the instructions. For example, upper left becomes upper right, and so on.

Pressing

Pressing is crucial to the success of pieced tri-angles. Nothing will do more to improve your piecing than good pressing technique.

It's important to press fabric before you cut. Pressing out wrinkles after cutting can skew triangles dramatically. The angles in this book are precise, and adding or subtracting even a few degrees can lead to problems.

One of the difficulties associated with any block that brings a lot of points together is bulk. As a hand quilter, I prefer to press seam allowances to one side rather than open. To minimize bulk, I do my "Chubby Checker" or "twist" press. I press the seam allowance toward the darker fabric, then open just the ends, where the seam will meet others. This creates a little fold or twist in the seam allowance. Don't worry, it will not mar the final product. Piecing is most accurate when the seams are open at bulky intersections.

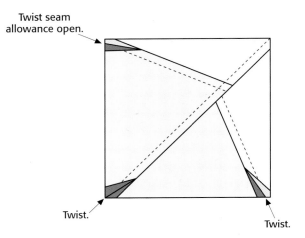

Twist seam allowance open.

Twist.

Twist.

You can press seam allowances to one side so that they butt up against adjoining seams; however, this creates bulky areas that you will want to trim. I use this method on the Basic block Wing seams, because only two seams are involved.

Of course, if you are a machine quilter, you can press the entire seam open. I have even pressed seams open on hand-quilted wall hangings, but I wouldn't on a bed quilt because an open seam isn't as strong as one that is pressed to one side. If you do press the seams open, remember that any in-the-ditch quilting will have to be done in the seam, right over the stitching.

Whichever method you choose, press the segment gently so as not to skew it, and make sure to press the seam along its entire length. Always keep in mind that the object of pressing is to make the fabric lie flat. If you return to the machine and the block is misbehaving, go back and press it again. A light spray starch can help.

Matching

I learned to appreciate pins during this adventure, especially when seam allowances were pressed to one side and lying on top of each other (when I elected not to "twist" press). Bulky seam intersections can occur in Basic block construction when the positions of the light and dark fabrics force you to press adjoining seams in the same direction.

Align the seams, stacking all four seam allowances. Place a pin parallel to the seam, as close to the stitching as possible.

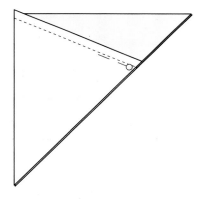

When joining blocks with bulky intersections, use the paper trick. Align the seams, pinning as described previously. Align a piece of scrap paper with the edge of the fabric and sew a ¼" seam as usual, over the paper. The presser foot will slide over the bulky intersections without pushing the points out of alignment.

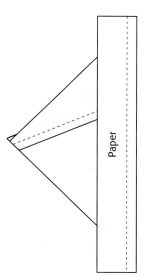

Remove the paper after finishing the seam. If you sew with a short stitch, the paper is easy to remove. When sewing long seams, use a scrap of paper to cover each bulky area as you come to it.

The more I piece, the more I like the paper trick. Once the blocks are trimmed and the points are in the proper position, pinning the seams is not a problem and there is no need to watch as you sew the blocks together. In fact, I am sure that sewing "blind" is an aid because it removes the temptation to alter the seam path.

NOTE: Do not use newspaper for the paper trick—the ink rubs off. Any other paper will do, though. Think of the junk mail you can eliminate from your countertop!

SIMPLY STELLAR SAMPLER

Finished size: 48" x 56"
Building block size: 4" x 4"
Star block size: 8" x 8"

The Simply Stellar Sampler incorporates all the different blocks in this book. Once you've made the sampler, you'll be ready to take on any of the other projects with confidence.

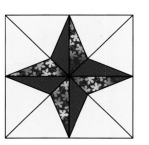

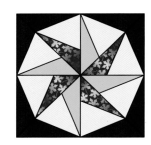

Basic Block **Basic Star** **Pinwheel Block** **Pinwheel Star**

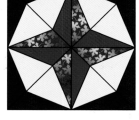
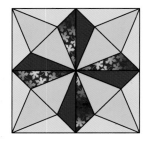

Pieced Diamond Block **Pieced Diamond Star** **Diamond Star Variation**

SIMPLY STELLAR SAMPLER by Mary Sue Suit, 1998, Alliance, Nebraska, 48" x 56". All the piecing is accomplished with two simple triangle shapes.

Materials (44"-wide cotton)

1 yd.   Fabric A (medium-dark) for star points
¾ yd.   Fabric B (medium-dark) for star points
1½ yds. Fabric C (light) for background
¾ yd.   Fabric D (medium-light) for background
¾ yd.   Fabric E (medium) for star points
2½ yds. Fabric F (dark) for background, outer border,
            and binding
½ yd.   Fabric G (medium gradated) for pieced
            inner border (or 1¾ yds. if you prefer
            not to piece the border)

TIP

• As you work through the sampler, save your leftover strips and use them for the next step.
• Cut a 1" square of each fabric, glue the squares to an index card, and label them "Fabric A," "Fabric B," and so on. This will be especially helpful if your color scheme differs from the one in the photo.

Lesson One: The Basic Block

Basic Block

Finished block size: 4" x 4"

Cutting

From Fabric A, cut:
   4 strips, each 2" x the width of the fabric

From Fabric B, cut:
   4 strips, each 2" x the width of the fabric

From Fabric C, cut:
   6 strips, each 4" x the width of the fabric

TROUBLESHOOTING TIP: To keep the outer edges of the Basic block on the straight of grain, you need to cut a mirror-image pair of each triangle.

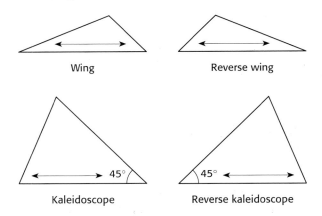

If you want to cut both the regular and reversed shapes from the same fabric, simply leave the fabric folded in half when you finish cutting your crosswise strips, then cut your shapes from the layered fabric. You'll have one regular and one reversed shape. If you need to cut many wings from the same fabric, place two strips same sides together.

NOTE: When using two different fabrics, layer the strips with same sides together and always cut with the same fabric on top.

Wings

TEMPLATE METHOD

1. Place 1 Fabric A strip on 1 Fabric B strip, right sides together.

2. Place the 2" Wing template (page 92) on the fabric strips, aligning the long side of the template with the bottom edge of the strips and placing the point of the 45-degree angle just inside the selvage. Cut around the template. This placement wastes the least fabric and gets rid of the selvage.

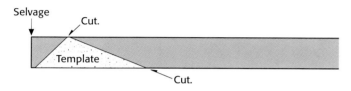

3. Without moving the fabric strips, rotate the template, aligning the longest edge with the top of the strip and the next-longest edge with the previous cut. Cut along the short edge. Proceed with step 4 at right.

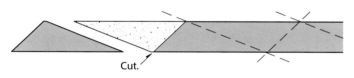

MARY SUE'S TRIANGLE RULER METHOD

1. Place 1 Fabric A strip on 1 Fabric B strip, right sides together.

2. With the center line of the ruler horizontal and the 90-degree angle pointing left, place the 2" marking at the bottom edge of the fabric, just inside the selvage. Cut around the ruler.

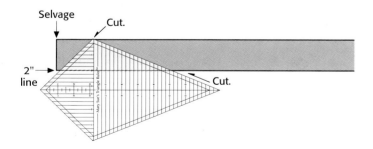

3. Without moving the fabric strips, rotate the ruler, aligning the 2" marking on the ruler with the top of the strip, and the other long edge with the previous cut. Cut along the short edge.

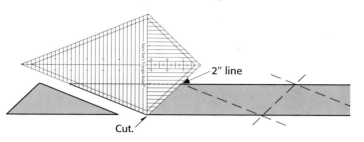

4. Continue rotating the ruler (or template) to cut 32 Wing sets from the Fabric A and B strips. Always cut the fabrics with the right sides together and fabric A on top. Make a notation to help you remember.

Straight-Grain Kaleidoscope Triangle Sets

TROUBLESHOOTING TIP: For Basic blocks, one long edge of each Kaleidoscope triangle needs to be on the straight grain. Be sure to lay the Kaleidoscope template on the fabric strip so that one long side aligns with the edge of the strip, as shown below, or use Mary Sue's Triangle Ruler as described on page 16.

TEMPLATE METHOD

1. Place 2 Fabric C strips same sides together.

2. Place the 5¼" Kaleidoscope template (page 92) on the strips just inside the selvage, aligning one long side of the template with the upper edge of the strip. Cut along the template.

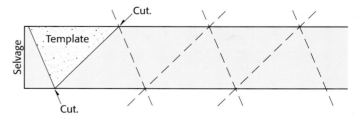

3. Without moving the fabric strips, rotate the template so that the long edge that was at the top for the last cut is at the bottom. Cut along the template.

4. Continue rotating the template to cut 32 Kaleidoscope sets from the Fabric C strips.

TIP

If you have trouble recognizing the straight-grain edge of cut triangles, mark both long edges of the fabric strip with a soap sliver or piece of chalk before you cut.

MARY SUE'S TRIANGLE RULER METHOD

1. Place 2 Fabric C strips same sides together.

2. Place the 45-degree-angle tip at the top of the fabric strips and align the center line of the ruler with the selvage. Make sure the center line is perpendicular to the cut edge of the strips. Cut along the ruler to establish the correct angle.

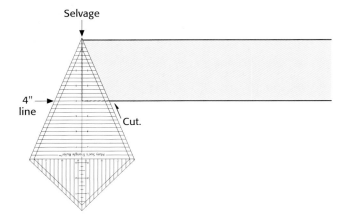

3. Align the crossbar with the previous cut as shown and place the 112.5-degree angle at the bottom edge of the fabric strips. Cut along the ruler.

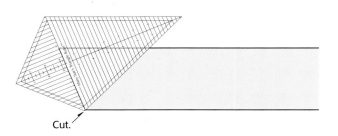

4. Align the crossbar with the previous cut and slide the ruler down so the 112.5-degree angle is at the top of the fabric strips. Cut along the ruler.

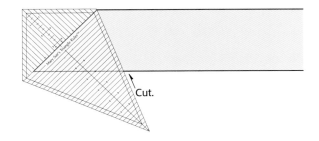

5. Continue across the strip to cut 32 Kaleidoscope sets from the Fabric C strips.

Block Assembly

TROUBLESHOOTING TIP: The Basic block will stretch too easily if you place the bias grain at the edges. To make sure the straight grain of the fabric winds up at the outer edge, lay out the pieces for each block before you stitch, paying special attention to grain line.

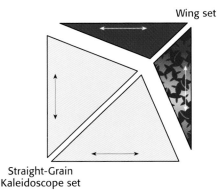

Wing set

Straight-Grain
Kaleidoscope set

1. With the Wing on top, sew a right Wing triangle to a right Kaleidoscope triangle as shown. Position the point of the Kaleidoscope so that it extends beyond the Wing. Always sew from the 112.5-degree end of the Wing triangle toward the

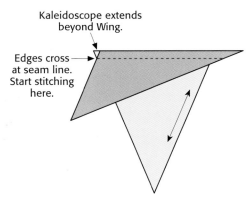

skinny end, and use a ¼" seam allowance. The first stitch should go through both fabrics. Press the seam allowances toward the Wing, or try the twist press (page 10).

TROUBLESHOOTING TIP: When properly positioned, the point of the Kaleidoscope extends beyond the Wing, the edges cross at the seam line, and the long skinny corner of the Wing extends well beyond the other corner of the Kaleidoscope. *Ignore the extra fabric.* You will trim the corner in a later step.

2. Repeat for the left Wing and Kaleidoscope triangles, starting with the Wing on the bottom and pressing toward the Kaleidoscope.

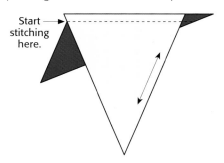

Start stitching here.

3. With right sides together, pin the pieced sections together along the long edge. The seam allowances should butt up against each other. Stitch. Press the seam allowances to one side. Throughout the project, always press this seam toward the same side (the same Wing fabric).

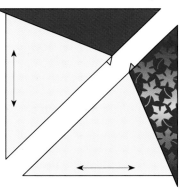

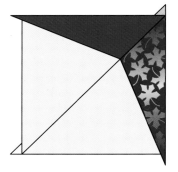

Trimming

If you didn't offset your pieces properly, trimming will fix the problem. You'll get perfect points every time.

1. Place the Basic block on the cutting mat with the Wing corner at lower left.

2. Lay a square ruler on the block with 0 at upper right. Align the ruler's diagonal line with the center seam, and place the 4⅜" marks at the Wing triangle seams. Trim any excess from the upper and right-hand edges of the block.

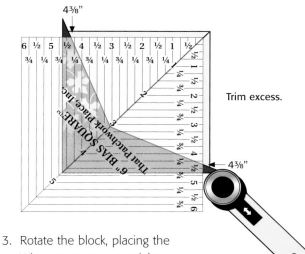

4⅜"

Trim excess.

4⅜"

3. Rotate the block, placing the Wing corner at upper right.

4. Lay your square ruler on the block with 0 at upper right. Align the ruler's diagonal line with the center seam, and align the 4½" marks with the bottom and left-hand edges of the block. Trim any excess from the upper and right-hand edges.

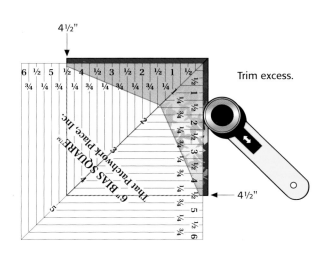

4½"

Trim excess.

4½"

5. Press, twisting the seams open at each corner (page 10).

You have completed 1 Basic block. Make 32 blocks.

Basic Star Block

1. Using 4 Basic blocks, lay out the Basic Star block. Sew 2 rows of 2 blocks. Press, twisting open both ends of each seam.

2. Join the rows. Press, twisting open both ends of the seam. Make 4 blocks.

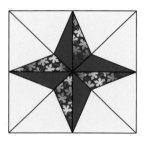

Make 4.

Filler Block

1. Using 4 Basic blocks, lay out the Filler block. Sew 2 rows of 2 blocks. Press, twisting open both ends of each seam. Join the rows. Press. Make 2 blocks.

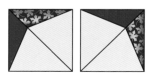

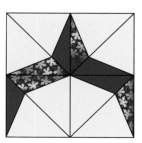

Make 2.

2. Join the Filler Blocks and 2 Basic Star blocks to make the middle row. Press, twisting open both ends of each seam.

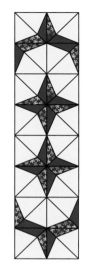

3. Use the remaining 8 Basic blocks to make 4 Filler pairs as shown. Press, twisting open both ends of each seam.

Make 2.

Make 2.

Mitered-Corner Blocks

Most of my quilts have miters somewhere. I like mitered borders, and I also frequently use what I call "miter corners," which are mitered sections within the pieced design.

Cutting

1. From Fabric D, cut 2 strips, each 4½" x the width of the fabric. Lay the strips right sides together and remove the selvages, using a ruler as shown to keep your cut perpendicular to the long edges.

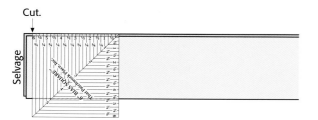

Cut.

Selvage

2. Measure 4¼" from the left-hand edge along the bottom of the strip, and make a mark.

3. Align the diagonal line of a square ruler with the upper edge of the fabric as shown below, and run the edge of the ruler through the mark on the fabric. Cut along the ruler as shown.

4. Measure 4¼" from the diagonal cut at the top of the strips. Mar, then cut perpendicular to the long edges, as shown below.

5. Repeat steps 2–4, referring to the illustration below and measuring 8¼" instead of 4¼".

NOTE: You can figure the measurements for mitered pieces yourself. For each miter, subtract ¼" from the unfinished size of the piece you are joining it to.

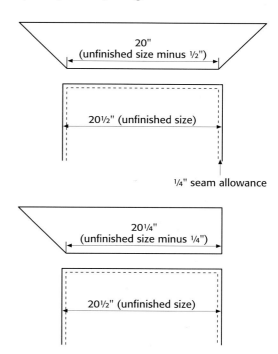

20"
(unfinished size minus ½")

20½" (unfinished size)

¼" seam allowance

20¼"
(unfinished size minus ¼")

20½" (unfinished size)

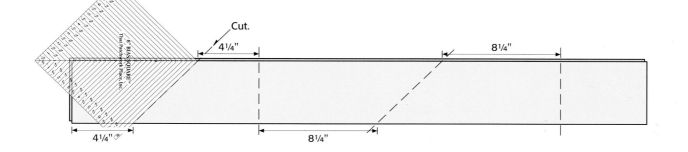

Cut.

4¼"

8¼"

4¼"

8¼"

8¼"

Block Assembly

1. Lay out the Mitered-Corner blocks in 2 sets of 2.

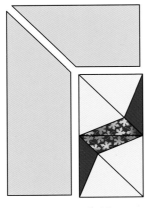 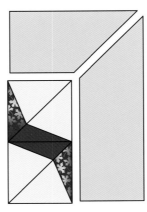

Lay out 2 "left."   Lay out 2 "right."

2. ***For right corners:*** With right sides together, lay the 8¼" miter piece on the pieced unit as shown. The pieced unit should extend beyond the miter piece at the miter cut.

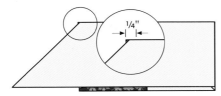

1/4"

   For left corners: With right sides together, lay the 4¼" miter piece on the pieced unit as shown, matching the straight-cut end with the long edge of the pieced unit.

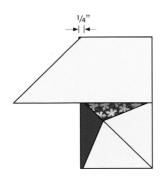

1/4"

3. Using a ¼" seam allowance, sew the pieces together, beginning ¼" from the edge of the pieced unit. Do not press.

4. Sew a 4¼" miter piece to the short side of the right corner unit and an 8¼" piece to the left corner unit as shown. Start each seam at the straight edge and end it at the previous seam. Do not press.

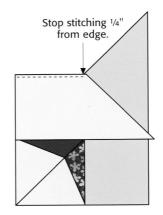

Stop stitching ¼" from edge.

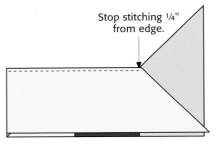

Stop stitching ¼" from edge.

5. With right sides together, fold the Basic block nearest the miter in half diagonally. Align the raw edges of the miter pieces. Sew the miter from the inside corner to the outside edge. Repeat for the remaining corner units.

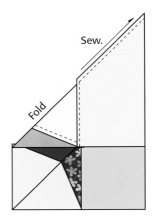

Sew.

Fold

6. Press the seam allowances from steps 3 and 4 toward the miter pieces. Allow the diagonal miter seam to lie in whatever direction it chooses.

7. Sew the corner units to the 2 remaining Basic Star blocks to form the side rows.

8. Join the side rows to the middle row. Use the resulting pieced section for the center of the Sampler or stop here for a wall hanging or table centerpiece.

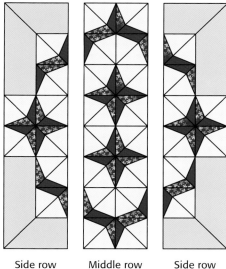

Side row   Middle row   Side row

Lesson Two: The Pinwheel Block

The Pinwheel block is another building block. The pinwheel spins because one pair of Wings points in the same direction, rather than in opposite directions. To get the Wings to point this way, you'll stack the strips same sides up instead of same sides together.

To make the Pinwheel block, you'll use Regular Kaleidoscope triangles for the first time. With these triangles, the straight of grain runs along the base—the short side. Regular Kaleidoscope triangles are a little easier to cut than the straight-grain variety.

Pinwheel Block

NOTE: For Regular Kaleidoscope triangles, the template size is equal to the strip width.

Building block size: 4"
Pinwheel Star block size: 8"

Cutting
From Fabric A, cut:
4 strips, each 2" x the width of the fabric

From Fabric E, cut:
4 strips, each 2" x the width of the fabric

From Fabric C, cut:
3 strips, each 4" x the width of the fabric

From Fabric F, cut:
7 strips, each 2" x the width of the fabric

TIP
Start with Fabric A and C strips left over from making the Basic blocks, then cut additional strips as needed.

Regular Kaleidoscope Triangle Sets

1. Place 1 Fabric A strip on 1 Fabric E strip, wrong sides up (the exception to the "same sides together" rule). Place the 2" Wing template or Mary Sue's Triangle Ruler on the fabric so that the skinny angle points right. Referring to "Wings" on page 15, cut Wing sets across the strips. Cut a total of 32 Wing sets from Fabrics A and E.

2. With the Fabric F strips same sides together—fold the seventh strip in half—cut 32 Wing sets.

3. Place 2 Fabric C strips same sides together. Leave the third strip folded. Trim the selvages as described on page 16. Using the 4" Kaleidoscope template (page 92) or Mary Sue's Triangle Ruler, cut 32 Regular Kaleidoscope sets as shown.

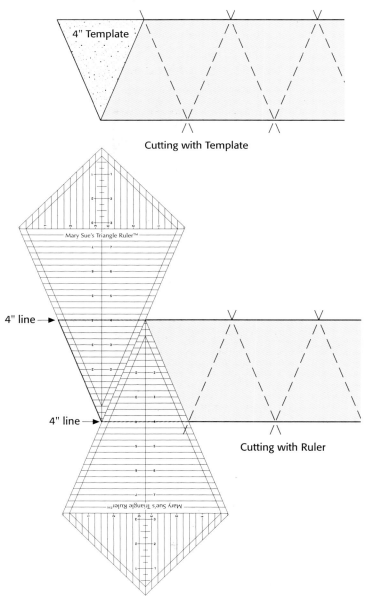

Cutting with Template

Cutting with Ruler

Block Assembly

1. Sew a star-point Wing (Fabric A or E) to each Regular Kaleidoscope triangle as shown. Press the seam allowances toward the Wing.

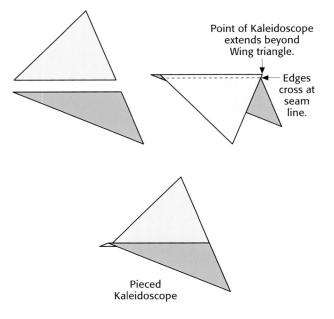

Point of Kaleidoscope extends beyond Wing triangle.

Edges cross at seam line.

Pieced Kaleidoscope

2. Trim each pieced Kaleidoscope to 4¾" as follows:
   Template Method: Make a 4¾" Kaleidoscope template, using the pattern on page 96. Cut a ¼" x ¼" notch at one base corner.

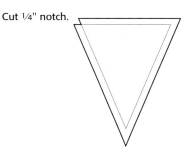

Cut ¼" notch.

Place the template on the pieced Kaleidoscope, with the Wing seam at the inside corner of the notch. Trim.

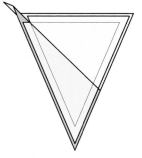

Trim excess.

Mary Sue's Ruler Method: Place the ruler on the Pieced Kaleidoscope so that the 4¾" line and the seam allowance line cross at the Wing seam. The 4¾" line should align with the short raw edge of the Pieced Kaleidoscope triangle. Trim as shown.

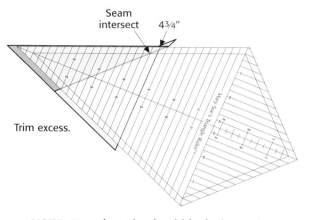

NOTE: For other Pinwheel block sizes, trim pieced Kaleidoscopes to the finished block size plus ¾".

3. Lay out the Pinwheel blocks, using 2 pieced Kaleidoscopes and 1 set of Fabric F Wings for each.

4. Sew the Fabric F Wings to the pieced Kaleidoscopes, positioning the point of the Kaleidoscope so that it extends beyond the Wing and the edges cross at the seam line. Trim the excess Wing tip from the Pieced Kaleidoscope to make positioning easier. Always sew from the wide end toward the skinny end. For Fabric A units, stitch with the Wing on top. For Fabric E units, stitch with the Kaleidoscope on top.

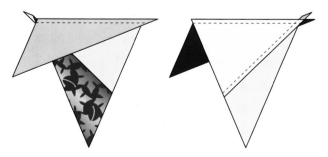

Always sew from wide end.

5. Press the seam allowances toward the Wings you just added. For the Fabric A star point, twist open the end of each seam when you press.

6. Trim the Fabric A half as shown.

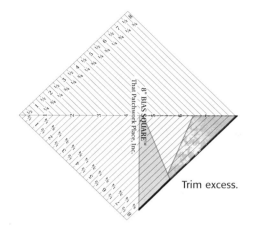

7. Matching the Fabric F Wing seams, sew a Fabric A unit to a Fabric E unit along the long edges to form a square. Press the seam allowances toward the Fabric E unit. Make 32.

Trimming

1. To trim the blocks to 4½", place each block on the mat with the star point Wings (Fabrics A and E) at upper right. Place a square ruler on the block, aligning the ruler's diagonal line with the diagonal seam and the 4⅜" marks with the Fabric F Wing seams. The Kaleidoscope point at lower right should hit the 4¼" mark and be ¼" from the edge of the ruler. Trim any excess.

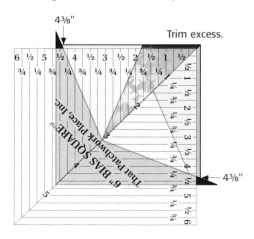

2. Rotate the block. Align the diagonal line on the ruler with the diagonal seam, and the lower left-hand corner with the 4½" mark. The Kaleidoscope point in the upper left-hand corner should hit the 4¼" mark. Trim any excess.

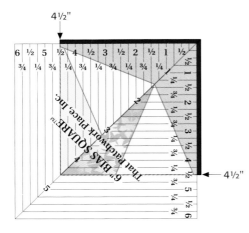

3. Press, twisting open the seams at the corners.

Pinwheel Star Block

Lay out 4 Pinwheel blocks to form a Pinwheel Star block. Sew the blocks into pairs, press, then join the pairs. Press. Make 8 blocks.

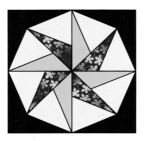

Pinwheel Star
Make 8.

Lesson Three: The Pieced Diamond Block

The Pieced Diamond block is made up of two Wing sets and one Regular Kaleidoscope set. It is similar to the Pinwheel block.

Pieced Diamond
Block

Block size: 4" x 4"

Cutting

For instructions on cutting Wing sets, refer to page 15; for Regular Kaleidoscope sets, page 22. Use the 2" Wing and 4" Kaleidoscope templates on page 92, or use Mary Sue's Triangle Ruler.

From Fabric A, cut:
    2 strips, each 2" x the width of the fabric, for Wing sets

From Fabric B, cut:
    2 strips, each 2" x the width of the fabric, for Wing sets

From Fabric F, cut:
    4 strips, each 2" x the width of the fabric, for Wing sets

From Fabric C, cut:
    1 strip, 4" x the width of the fabric, for Regular Kaleidoscope sets

1. Place the Fabric A and Fabric B strips same sides together and cut 16 sets of 2" Wings.

2. Place the Fabric F strips same sides together and cut 16 sets of 2" Wings.

3. Leave the Fabric C strip folded and cut 16 sets of 4" Regular Kaleidoscopes.

Block Assembly

1. Select 1 Fabric A/B Wing set, 1 Fabric C Kaleidoscope set, and 1 Fabric F Wing set. Lay out the pieces as shown below.

2. Beginning with the Fabric F Wings, join a Wing to a long side of each Kaleidoscope triangle to form a pieced Kaleidoscope (page 22). Press the seam allowances toward the darker fabric.

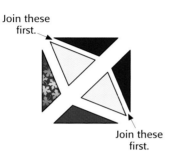

Join these first.

Join these first.

3. Use your trimming template (page 22) or Mary Sue's Triangle Ruler to trim the resulting triangles to 4³⁄₄", with the Wing seam at ¹⁄₄" as shown below. The Wings in one triangle will point to the left; the Wings in the other triangle will point to the right.

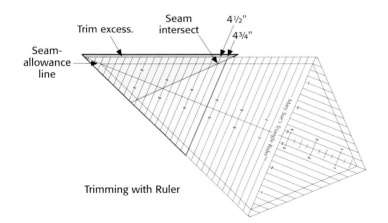

Trim excess.

Seam intersect

4¹⁄₂"

4³⁄₄"

Seam-allowance line

Trimming with Ruler

NOTE: For Pieced Diamond blocks with a finished size smaller than 5" square, trim pieced Kaleidoscopes to the size of the finished block plus ³⁄₄". For blocks 5" or larger, trim to the finished block size plus ¹⁄₂".

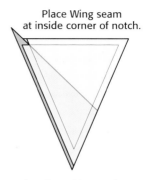

Place Wing seam at inside corner of notch.

Trimming with Template

4. Sew the Fabric A and B Wings to the pieced Kaleidoscopes, positioning the point of the Kaleidoscope so that it extends beyond the Wing and edges cross at the seam line. Always sew from the wide end toward the skinny end. The skinny ends of the Wings will cross.

5. Join the resulting triangles, matching the seams. Experiment with pinning (page 11) and twist-pressing (page 10) to find the piecing method you prefer. Make 16.

Add A and B Wings.

Trimming

1. Place your square ruler on a block, with the corner formed by the pieced Kaleidoscope at upper right. Align the ruler's diagonal line with the center seam and the 4 1/4" marks with the diamond points. Trim any excess.

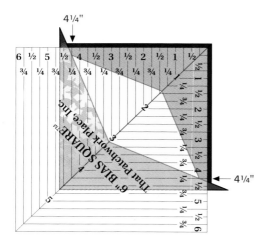

2. Rotate the block, placing the corner you just trimmed at lower left. Align the ruler's 4 1/2" marks with the edges you just cut and the diagonal line with the center seam. Check that the 4 1/4" marks hit the diamond points and trim any excess.

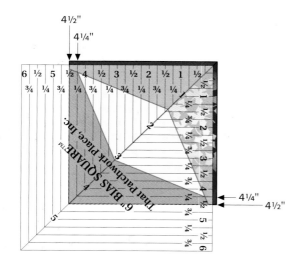

3. Press, twisting open the seams at the corners.

4. Repeat steps 1–3 for each block.

Pieced Diamond Star Block

Lay out 4 Pieced Diamond blocks to make a Pieced Diamond Star block. Sew the blocks into pairs, press, then join the pairs. Press. Make 4 blocks.

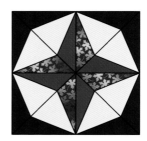

Pieced Diamond Star
Make 4.

Pieced Diamond Star Variation

For instructions on cutting Wing sets, refer to page 15; for Regular Kaleidoscope sets, page 22. Use the 2" Wing and 4" Kaleidoscope templates on page 92, or use a Mary Sue's Triangle Ruler.

From Fabric A, cut:
3 strips, each 2" x the width of the fabric, for Wing sets

From Fabric B, cut:
3 strips, each 2" x the width of the fabric, for Wing sets

From Fabric D, cut:
5 strips, each 2" x the width of the fabric, for Wing sets

From Fabric E, cut:
3 strips, each 4" x the width of the fabric, for Regular Kaleidoscope sets

1. Place the Fabric A and Fabric B strips same sides together and cut 24 sets of 2" Wings.

2. Place the Fabric D strips same sides together and cut 24 sets of 2" Wings.

3. Place the Fabric E strips same sides together and cut 24 sets of 4" Regular Kaleidoscopes.

Block Assembly

1. For each block, select 1 Fabric A/B Wing set, one Fabric E Kaleidoscope set, and 1 Fabric D Wing set. Lay out 24 Pieced Diamond blocks.

2. Referring to "Block Assembly" on page 25, assemble and trim the blocks. Add the Fabric A and B Wings first.

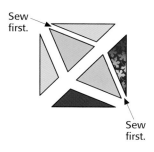

3. Lay out the Pieced Diamond blocks to form 6 Pieced Diamond Star Variation blocks. Join the blocks and press.

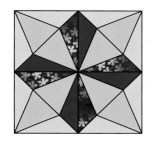

Pieced Diamond Star Variation
Make 6.

NOTE: The Pieced Diamond Star Variation is the most difficult block to match exactly. The paper trick (page 11) really helps.

Sampler Assembly

1. Join blocks into rows as shown, press, and sew the rows to the top and bottom of the Sampler center. Press toward the Sampler center.

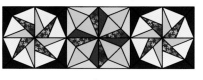

Make 2.

2. Join blocks into rows as shown, press, and sew the rows to the sides of the Sampler center. Press toward the Sampler center.

Make 2.

Inner Border

I used a gradated fabric for my inner border, which I pieced so that it was dark in the corners and light in the center.

From Fabric G, cut:

8 strips, each 2" x the width of the fabric; join the strips in pairs, end to end, to make 4 pieced strips

1. For the top and bottom borders, fold 2 of the pieced border strips in half crosswise at the seam. On each strip, measure 20" from the stitching line, mark, and cut a 45-degree angle (page 19).

2. Repeat for the side borders, measuring 24" from the stitching line.

3. Referring to "Adding Borders" on page 87, sew the border strips to the quilt top. Press the seam allowances toward the border.

A STELLAR OPTION by Mary Sue Suit, 1996, Alliance, Nebraska, 48" x 60". This is where my triangle journey began—surely somewhere near the middle. Use the work sheet on page 29 to explore a multitude of sampler options.

Outer Border and Binding

From Fabric F, cut:

2 *lengthwise* strips, each 3" x 50"

2 *lengthwise* strips, each 3" x 60"

2½"-wide bias strips as needed for binding

1. Fold the top and bottom borders in half cross-wise. Measure 21½" from the fold, mark, and cut a 45-degree angle.

2. Repeat step 1 for the side borders, measuring 25½" from the fold.

3. Referring to step 8 on page 87, sew the border strips to the quilt top. Press the seam allowances toward the border.

Finishing

Quilting and binding directions begin on page 88.

Simply Stellar Sampler Work Sheet

If you enlarged the building blocks to 5" and added the border shown below, the finished quilt would measure 90" x 100". There are many other ways to enlarge the Sampler. For example, 6" building blocks would yield a 60" x 72" Sampler top, without borders.

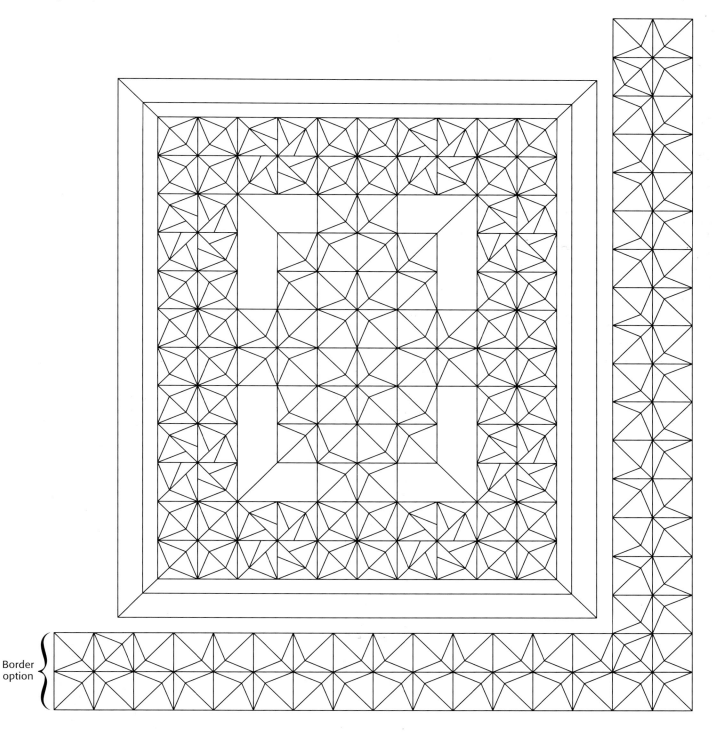

Border option

BASIC BLOCK PROJECTS

If you haven't made the Simply Stellar Sampler, be sure to work through "Lesson One: The Basic Block" (pages 14–18) before making any of the Basic block projects. Use scraps and cut and piece just a few of the shapes described. You don't need to cut all the strips and piece all the blocks required for the Sampler.

All the quilts in this section are based on the Basic block. Simple color manipulation gives you endless options, and rearranging the blocks allows you to form stars, hearts, and octagons. Something unexpected is sure to develop if you take charge of your quilt and try the "what happens if" approach to design.

TWINKLE, TWINKLE ALLOVER STAR

Quilt size: 28" x 36"
Building block size: 2"
Basic Star block size: 4"

In this design, color and value define areas of the quilt. To enlarge the quilt, simply make bigger blocks. The same quilt plan made with 6" blocks would measure 84" x 108".

 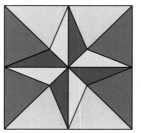 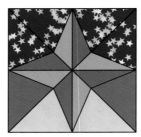 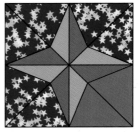

TWINKLE, TWINKLE ALLOVER STAR by Mary Sue Suit, 1998, Alliance, Nebraska, 28" x 36".

Materials (44"-wide cotton)

¼ yd. dark brown for stars

¼ yd. gold for stars

⅜ yd. medium-light brown for stars

⅜ yd. medium-dark brown for stars

¾ yd. light blue for background

⅝ yd. medium blue for background

¾ yd. dark print for background and border

1 fat quarter brown plaid for binding

Cutting

For instructions on cutting Wing sets, refer to page 15; for Straight-Grain Kaleidoscope sets, pages 15–16. Use the 1¼" Wing and 3" Straight-Grain Kaleidoscope templates on page 90, or use Mary Sue's Triangle Ruler.

From the dark brown, cut:

5 strips, each 1¼" x the width of the fabric

From the gold, cut:

5 strips, each 1¼" x the width of the fabric; place the dark brown and gold strips right sides together (always place the dark brown on top) and cut 80 sets of 1¼" Wings from the strips

From the medium-light brown, cut:

6 strips, each 1¼" x the width of the fabric

From the medium-dark brown, cut:

6 strips, each 1¼" x the width of the fabric; place the medium-light and medium-dark brown strips right sides together (always place the darker fabric on top) and cut 96 sets of 1¼" Wings from the strips

From the light blue, cut:

7 strips, each 2¼" x the width of the fabric; cut 76 sets of 3" Straight-Grain Kaleidoscopes from the strips

2 squares, each 4⅞" x 4⅞"

From the medium blue, cut:

5 strips, each 2¼" x the width of the fabric; cut 48 sets of 3" Straight-Grain Kaleidoscopes from the strips

2 squares, each 4⅞" x 4⅞"

From the dark print, cut:

5 strips, each 2¼" x the width of the fabric; cut 52 sets of 3" Straight-Grain Kaleidoscopes from the strips

4 strips, each 2½" x the width of the fabric

From the brown plaid, cut:

2½"-wide bias strips as needed for binding

Block Assembly

1. Referring to "Block Assembly" on pages 16–18, make the blocks shown below. As you arrange the pieces, make sure the straight grain is on the outer edge. Trim each block to 2½" x 2½", with the Wing seam at 2⅜" (page 17).

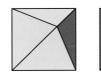

Make 32.   Make 24.    Make 24.

Make 20.    Make 20.    Make 52. 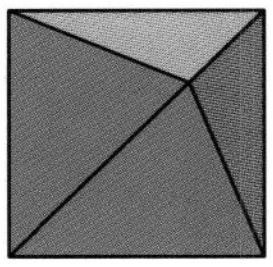   Make 4.

2. Join sets of 4 Basic blocks to make Basic Star blocks.

 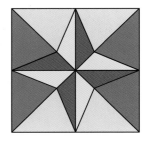

Make 8.   Make 12.

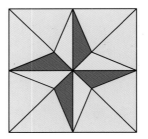 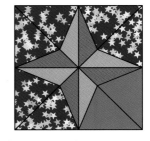

Make 20.   Make 4.

3. Place a light blue 4⅞" square and a medium blue 4⅞" square right sides together. Draw a diagonal line from corner to corner, using a ruler to make an accurate line.

4. Sew ¼" from the line on each side. Cut along the line, open, and press. Repeat with the other 2 squares to make a total of 4 pieced blocks.

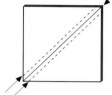

Mark and cut.

Sew.

Quilt Top Assembly

1. Referring to the illustration at right, lay out the quilt top. Sew the blocks into rows. Press.

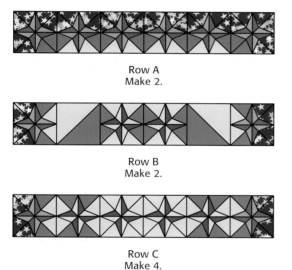

Row A
Make 2.

Row B
Make 2.

Row C
Make 4.

2. Join the rows. Press.

Border

1. Measure your quilt top. If it does not measure 24½" x 32½", refer to "Adding Borders" on page 87 to calculate one-half the finished size.

2. Fold your border strips in half crosswise. For the top and bottom borders, measure 12" (or your result from step 1) from the fold and mark. For the side borders, measure 16" (or your result from step 1) from the fold and mark.

Position a square ruler at the mark as shown, and cut a 45-degree-angle.

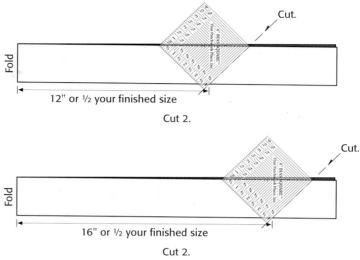

Cut.

Fold

12" or ½ your finished size

Cut 2.

Cut.

Fold

16" or ½ your finished size

Cut 2.

3. Referring to step 8 on page 87, sew the border strips to the quilt top. Press the seam allowances toward the border.

Finishing

Quilting and binding directions begin on page 88.

PLAYING WITH PURPLE

Quilt size: 40" x 40"
Building block size: 3"
Basic Star block size: 6"

This wall hanging is great with scraps. The background fabrics create fabulous secondary and tertiary designs. Be sure to include lots of contrast, from lightest lights to deepest darks.

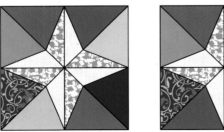

PLAYING WITH PURPLE by Mary Sue Suit, 1998, Alliance, Nebraska, 40" x 40".

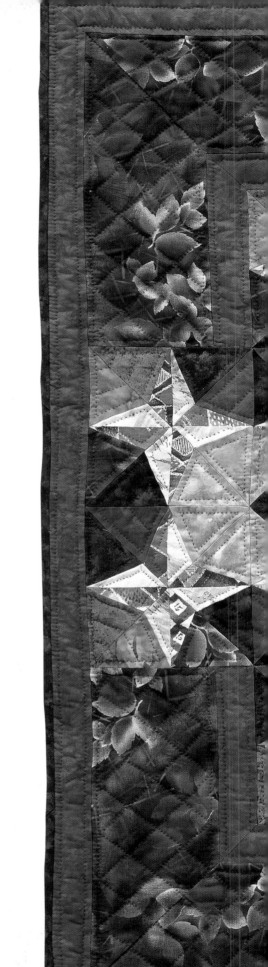

Materials (44"-wide cotton)

½ yd.   light print for stars
½ yd.   medium print for stars
¼ yd.   light pink for background
¼ yd.   lavender for background
¼ yd.   medium-light teal for background
¼ yd.   medium teal for background
¾ yd.   medium purple for background, miter pairs, and border
¼ yd.   dark purple for background
1⅛ yds.   medium blue floral for background, miter pairs, and binding
¼ yd.   dark blue for background

Cutting

For instructions on cutting Wing sets, refer to pages 15–16; for Straight-Grain Kaleidoscope sets, page 16. Use the 1½" Wing and 4" Straight-Grain Kaleidoscope templates on page 91, or use Mary Sue's Triangle Ruler.

From the light print, cut:

6 strips, each 1½" x the width of the fabric

From the medium print, cut:

6 strips, each 1½" x the width of the fabric. Pair the light and medium strips right sides together and cut 96 light/medium print Wing sets (light print on top).

From each background fabric, cut:

3 strips, each 3" x the width of the fabric, for a total of 24 strips

Pair strips of the same color family (2 pinks, 2 purples, etc.) right sides together and cut:

24 pink/lavender Straight-Grain Kaleidoscope sets (lavender on top)

24 teal Straight-Grain Kaleidoscope sets (medium teal on top)

24 purple Straight-Grain Kaleidoscope sets (medium purple on top)

24 blue Straight-Grain Kaleidoscope sets (medium blue floral on top)

From the remaining medium purple, cut:

6 strips, each 2" x the width of the fabric

From the remaining medium blue floral, cut:

2 strips, each 5" x 42", for miter pairs. If your fabric does not measure at least 42" across after preshrinking and removing selvages, cut 3 strips.

2½"-wide bias strips as needed for binding

Block Assembly

1. Referring to "Block Assembly" on pages 16–18, make the blocks shown below. As you arrange the pieces, make sure the straight grain is on the outer edge. Trim each block to 3½" x 3½", with the Wing seam at 3⅜" (page 17).

Make 8.   Make 8.   Make 24.

Make 16.   Make 16.   Make 24.

2. Lay out 24 Basic Star blocks. Stitch and press.

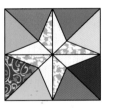 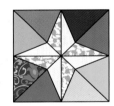

Basic Star A   Basic Star B
Make 8.   Make 16.

Unit I

1. Place 2 medium purple 2"-wide strips same sides together and remove the selvages. At the bottom of the strip, measure 6¼" from the left-hand edge and mark. At the mark, cut a 45-degree angle. From the diagonal cut, measure 6¼" along the top of the strip, mark, and cut straight across the strip as shown. Repeat to cut a total of 4 miter pairs.

Repeat with the 5"-wide medium
blue floral strips, cutting at 7¾".
If you have to use 3 strips,
cut 3 pairs from the first 2 strips,
then fold the third strip
in half and cut 1 pair.

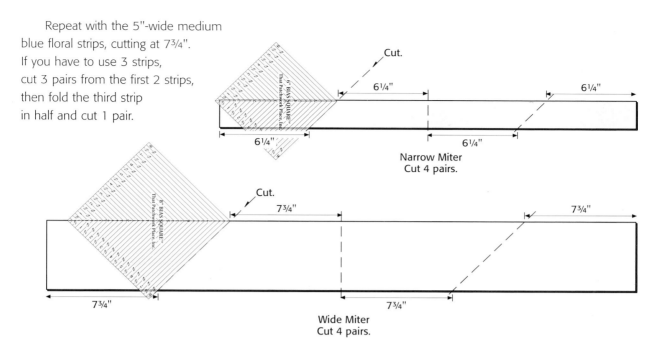

Narrow Miter
Cut 4 pairs.

Wide Miter
Cut 4 pairs.

2. Referring to "Block Assembly" on pages 20–21,
   sew the miter corners to Basic Star block B,
   sewing the narrow purple miters first and then
   adding the wide blue miters. This is Unit 1.
   Make 4.

Unit 1
Make 4.

Units 2 and 3

Assemble the remaining Star blocks into units as
shown below.

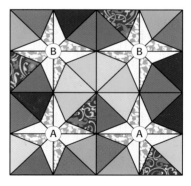

Unit 2
Make 4.

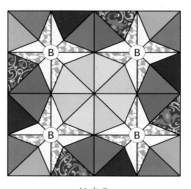

Unit 3
Make 1.

Quilt Top Assembly

Referring to the illustration below, lay out the quilt. Sew the units into rows. Press. Join the rows. Press.

Border

1. Referring to page 87, measure your quilt top and calculate one-half the finished size. Fold one of the remaining 2" purple strips in half crosswise.

   At the bottom edge of the strip, mark 18" (or half your finished size if different) from the fold. Cut a 45-degree angle at the mark. Repeat to make 4 border strips.

2. Referring to step 8 on page 87, sew the border strips to the quilt top. Press the seam allowances toward the border.

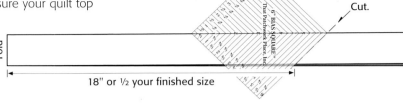

Border
Make 4.

Finishing

Quilting and binding directions begin on page 88.

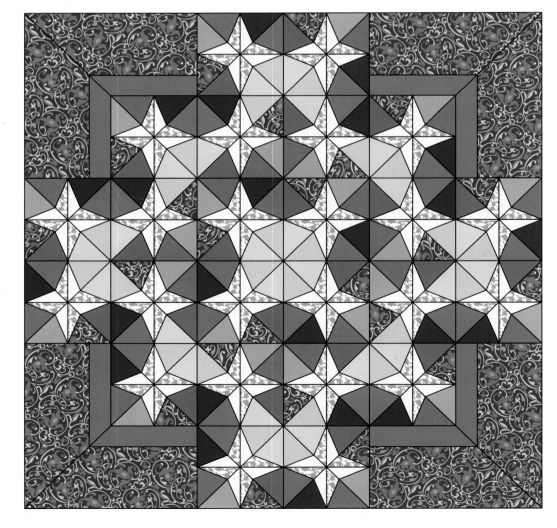

Allover Star Work Sheet

CLAMSHELL

Finished size: 70" x 90"
Building block size: 5"
Clamshell block size: 10"

I am very fond of this clamshell design. It is my updated version of the classic, without any curved piecing or appliqué. If you have a book containing clamshell quilts, take a look at the design options. You can make diagonal or straight rows of color, or radiating diamonds, to name a few possibilities.

This quilt takes some planning. Because the clamshell fabrics interlock, each block is different. Either make a color chart and follow it, or cut your fabrics and lay everything out and then piece each block. I am a "cut now, design as you go" person, so everything I do has an air of serendipity to it.

Clamshell is perfect for a twin-size bed. It is a wonderful project because the piecing is relatively easy and it goes fast. This would be a terrific flannel quilt to send off to school or to be loved to death on chilly nights. A smaller version would make a delightful baby quilt. The same design made with 3" blocks yields a 42" x 54" quilt.

CLAMSHELL by Mary Sue Suit, 1998, Alliance, Nebraska, 70" x 90".
Choose a large-scale print for the border, then pull colors from it for the clamshells.

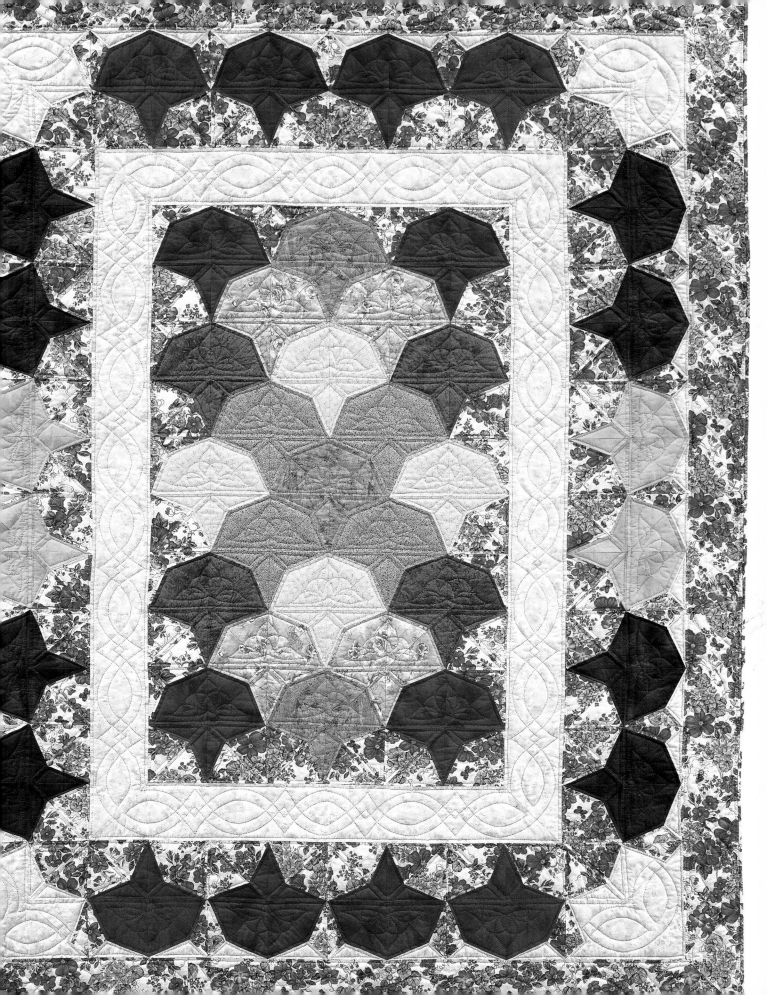

Materials (44"-wide cotton)

5 yds. large-scale floral for clamshells, outer border, and binding

2½ yds. light peach for inner border and blocks

⅞ yd. maroon for clamshells

½ yd. each of 5 medium fabrics for inner clamshells*

½ yd. each of 4 dark fabrics for outer clamshells*

*The ½-yard cuts are generous, to allow for cutting mistakes.

Cutting

For instructions on cutting Wing sets, refer to page 15; for Straight-Grain Kaleidoscope sets, pages 15–16. Use the 2¼" Wing and 5¾" Straight-Grain Kaleidoscope templates on page 94, or use Mary Sue's Triangle Ruler.

From the floral print, cut:

2 *lengthwise* strips, each 5½" x 95"

2 *lengthwise* strips, each 5½" x 75"

18 *crosswise* strips, each 2¼" x the width of the fabric; cut 38 sets of 2¼" Wings from the strips

12 *crosswise* strips, each 4½" x the width of the fabric; cut 58 sets of 5¾" Straight-Grain Kaleidoscopes from the strips

2½"-wide bias strips as needed for binding

From the peach, cut:

2 *lengthwise* strips, each 5½" x 65"

2 *lengthwise* strips, each 5½" x 45"

12 *crosswise* strips, each 2¼" x the width of the fabric; cut 24 sets of 2¼" Wings from the strips

2 *crosswise* strips, each 4½" x the width of the fabric; cut 4 sets of 5¾" Straight-Grain Kaleidoscopes from the strips

2 squares, each 11½" x 11½"

From the maroon, cut:

3 strips, each 2¼" x the width of the fabric; cut 16 sets of 2¼" Wings from the strips

4 strips, each 4½" x the width of the fabric; cut 16 sets of 5¾" Straight-Grain Kaleidoscopes from the strips

From *each* of the remaining clamshell fabrics, cut:

2 strips, each 2¼" x the width of the fabric; cut 8 sets of 2¼" Wings from the strips

2 strips, each 4½" x the width of the fabric; cut 8 sets of 5¾" Straight-Grain Kaleidoscopes from the strips

Block Assembly

1. Referring to "Block Assembly" on pages 16–18, make the blocks shown below. Trim each block to 5½" x 5½", with the Wing seam at 5⅜" (page 17).

Make 4. Make 40 (8 each of 5 clamshell fabrics). Make 20 (4 each of 5 clamshell fabrics). Make 20 (4 each of 5 clamshell fabrics).

2. Join the Basic blocks in sets of 4 to make 20 outer Clamshell blocks. Reserve the 4 floral/peach Basic blocks.

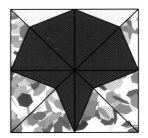

Outer Clamshell
Make 20
(4 each of
5 clamshell fabrics).

3. Referring to the illustration opposite for color placement, make 60 Basic blocks for the quilt center. Trim each block to 5½" x 5½", with the Wing seam at 5⅜".

4. Join the Basic blocks in sets of 4 to make 15 inner Clamshell blocks.

5. Sew the Clamshell blocks into 5 rows of 3 blocks each. Press. Join the rows. Press.

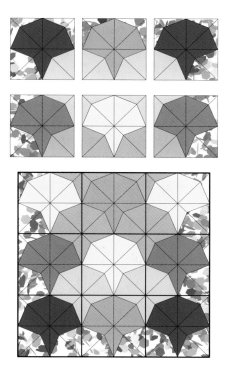

NOTE: You will have 2 Kaleidoscope sets and 2 Wing sets left over from 1 of your clamshell fabrics; discard these sets or save them for another project. You will also have 4 floral Wing sets and 4 peach Kaleidoscope sets left over. Reserve these for the Clamshell border.

Inner Border

1. Measure your quilt center. If it does not measure 30½" x 50½", refer to "Adding Borders" on page 87 to calculate one-half the finished size.

2. Fold the four 5½"-wide peach strips in half crosswise. On the 65"-long strips, measure 25" (or your length result from step 1) from the fold, mark, and cut a 45-degree angle (page 87). On the 45"-long strips, measure 15" (or your width result from step 1) from the fold, mark, and cut a 45-degree angle.

3. Referring to step 8 on page 87, sew the border strips to the quilt top. Press the seam allowances toward the border.

Clamshell Border

1. Sew the reserved floral Wings to the reserved peach Kaleidoscopes. To trim, lay a square ruler on the triangle, aligning the long edge of the triangle with the 5⅞" marks at the upper and right edges of the ruler and the Wing seam with the ⅛" mark as shown. Trim the upper and right edges. Make 4 right and 4 left half-blocks.

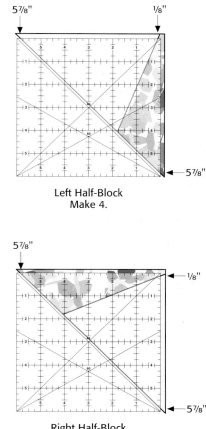

Left Half-Block
Make 4.

Right Half-Block
Make 4.

2. Sew 2 units from step 1 to each of the reserved floral/peach Basic blocks as shown. Press.

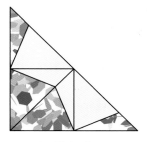

Make 4.

3. Cut the 11½" peach squares in half diagonally.

4. Place a peach triangle on a pieced triangle, right sides together. Using a ¼" seam allowance, stitch the pieces together along the long edge. Open the resulting square and press the seam allowances toward the large peach triangle. Trimming from the peach triangle only, trim to 10½" x 10½".

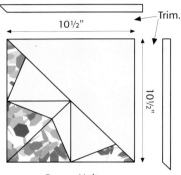

Corner Unit
Make 4.

5. Assemble the outer clamshells, referring to the photo on page 41. Use 6 clamshells for each side border. Use 4 clamshells and 2 corner units from step 4 for the top and bottom borders.

6. Sew the side borders to the quilt top; press. Add the top and bottom borders; press.

Outer Border

1. Measure your quilt top. If it does not measure 60½" x 80½", refer to "Adding Borders" on page 87 to calculate one-half the finished size.

2. Fold the 5½" floral strips in half crosswise. On the 95"-long strips, measure 40" (or your length result from step 1) from the fold, mark, and cut a 45-degree angle (page 87). On the 75"-long strips, measure 30" from the fold (or your width result from step 1), mark, and cut a 45-degree angle.

3. Referring to step 8 on page 87, sew the border strips to the quilt top. Press the seam allowances toward the border.

Finishing

Quilting and binding directions begin on page 88.

Clamshell Work Sheet

Traditional Heart Counterpane

Quilt size: 28" x 28"
Building block size: 2"

This small wall hanging introduces a heart shape made with Basic blocks. Fabrics in the photo quilt came from my scrap bag, and they range from medium-light pink to deep maroon. As with any scrap quilt, the more fabrics used, the more intriguing the design.

The Heart blocks are set on point with plain setting squares and triangles. To enlarge the quilt, just add more Heart blocks, squares, and triangles.

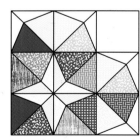 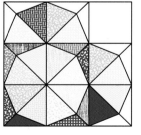

Traditional Heart Counterpane by Mary Sue Suit, 1998, Alliance, Nebraska, 28" x 28".

Materials (44"-wide cotton)

¼ yd. dark maroon

¾ yd. *total* assorted pink scraps for hearts and pieced border

¾ yd. white for Heart blocks and outer border

½ yd. pink floral for setting triangles and squares

½ yd. medium pink for inner border and binding

Cutting

For instructions on cutting Wing sets, refer to page 15; for Straight-Grain Kaleidoscope sets, pages 15–16. Use the 1¼" Wing and 3" Straight-Grain Kaleidoscope templates on page 90, or use Mary Sue's Triangle Ruler.

From the dark maroon, cut:

2 strips, each 1¼" x the width of the fabric; cut 16 sets of 1¼" Wings from the strips

From the assorted pink scraps and the remaining maroon, cut:

2¼"-wide light pink strips; the number of strips you need will depend on the width of your scraps. Cut 72 sets of 3" Straight-Grain Kaleidoscopes from the strips.

1¼"-wide strips from 2 of your lightest pinks; cut 4 sets of 1¼" Wings from each fabric

1¼"-wide strips from 2 of your dark pink or maroon fabrics; cut 4 sets of 1¼" Wings from each fabric

From the white, cut:

5 strips, each 1¼" x the width of the fabric; cut 40 sets of 1¼" Wings from the strips

8 squares, each 2½" x 2½"

4 strips, each 2½" x the width of the fabric

From the pink floral, cut:

1 square, 6½" x 6½"

2 squares, each 5½" x 5½"

1 square, 11" x 11"

From the medium pink, cut:

4 strips, each 2" x 24"

2½"-wide bias strips as needed for binding

Block Assembly

1. Referring to "Block Assembly" on pages 16–18, make the blocks shown below. Trim each block to 2½" x 2½", with the Wing seam at 2⅜" (page 17).

Make 8.   Make 24.   Make 8.

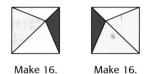

Make 16.   Make 16.

2. Using the Basic blocks and the white squares, lay out 4 Heart blocks as shown. Sew the pieces into rows. Press. Join the rows. Press, twisting open the ends of the seams.

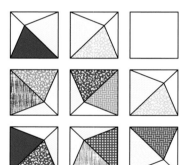

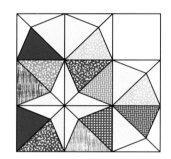

Star Heart
Make 2.

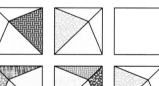

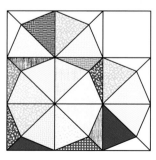

Circle Heart
Make 2.

3. Find the midpoint of each block edge and pin.

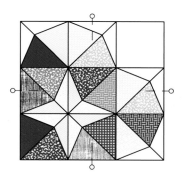

Quilt Center Assembly

1. Cut the 5½" floral squares in half diagonally and mark the midpoints of the long edges of the resulting triangles. Cut the 11" floral square in quarters on the diagonal. Mark the midpoints of the short sides of the resulting triangles.

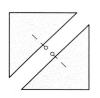

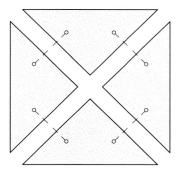

2. Lay out the quilt center as shown. Sew the Heart blocks and background pieces into 3 diagonal rows, being careful to match midpoints and seams. Press.

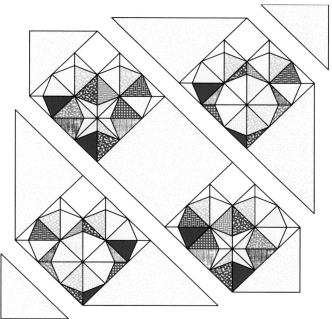

3. Trim the long sides of each row, cutting off the excess setting fabric.

4. Join the rows, then add the remaining corner triangles. Press.

5. Trim the top to measure 17½" x 17½", being careful to leave a ¼" seam allowance at the points of the Heart blocks.

Inner Border

1. Stack all 4 medium pink strips. Cut the left-hand edge at a 45-degree angle. Measure 17" from the left-hand edge along the bottom, mark, and cut a 45-degree angle.

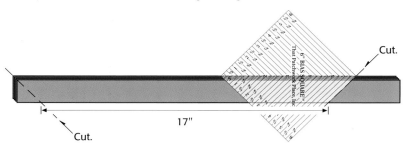

2. Referring to step 8 on page 87, sew the border strips to the quilt top. Press the seam allowances toward the border.

Pieced Border

1. Sew the remaining Basic blocks and 2½" white squares into border strips as shown.

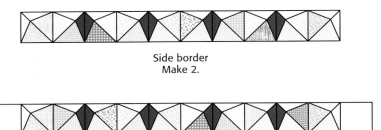

Side border
Make 2.

Top and bottom borders
Make 2.

2. Sew the side borders to the quilt top. Press the seam allowances toward the borders. Add the top and bottom borders. Press the seam allowances toward the borders.

Outer Border

1. Fold a 2½"-wide white strip in half crosswise. Measure 12" from the fold, mark, and cut a 45-degree angle (page 87). Repeat to cut 4 border strips.

Fold

Cut.

12"

Make 4.

2. Referring to step 8 on page 87, sew the border strips to the quilt top. Press the seam allowances toward the border.

Finishing

Quilting and binding directions begin on page 88.

RANDOM HEARTS by Karen Walker, 1998, Lakeside, Nebraska, 59" x 71". Karen used 2" blocks for the small hearts and 3" blocks for the large hearts. The floral background and inventive purple border bring it all together. Karen lives on a ranch in the Nebraska Sand Hills. Kids and cows keep Karen at home, so we usually have piecing lessons over the phone. She makes her quilts from stash fabrics—hence the name "Random Hearts."

HEARTS AND STARS

Quilt size: 34" x 34"
Building block sizes: Heart, 2"; Star and pieced border, 4¼"
Nine-patch unit: 8½"

This design sets the Heart block within a square, making it easy to combine with Star blocks. The wall hanging is set in a nine-patch format with an outer border of Basic blocks and rectangles. Notice the elegant circular pattern formed by the stars. Use the work sheet on page 57 to enlarge the project or change the color scheme. Try for the dramatic with bold colors, or make a great scrap quilt.

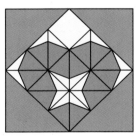
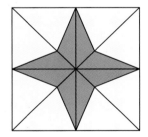

HEARTS AND STARS by Mary Sue Suit, 1998, Alliance, Nebraska, 34" x 34".

Materials (44"-wide cotton)

½ yd. dark pink
1⅛ yds. blue
1⅛ yds. light pink
1 fat quarter coordinating print for binding

Cutting

For instructions on cutting Wing sets, refer to page 15; for Straight-Grain Kaleidoscope sets, pages 15–16. For the Heart blocks, use the 1¼" Wing and 3" Straight-Grain Kaleidoscope templates on page 90; for the Stars and pieced border, use the 2" Wing and 5½" Straight-Grain Kaleidoscope templates on page 93; or use Mary Sue's Triangle Ruler.

From the dark pink, cut:

4 strips, each 2¼" x the width of the fabric; cut 40 sets of 3" Straight-Grain Kaleidoscopes from the strips

2 strips, each 2" x the width of the fabric

From the blue, cut:

2 strips, each 2" x the width of the fabric; place the 2"-wide blue and dark pink strips right sides together, dark pink on top, and cut 16 Wing sets

10 squares, each 5½" x 5½"

4 strips, each 4¼" x the width of the fabric; cut 16 sets of 5½" Straight-Grain Kaleidoscopes from the strips

4 rectangles, each 4¾" x 9"

From the light pink, cut:

5 strips, each 1¼" x the width of the fabric; cut 40 sets of 1¼" Wings from the strips

4 strips, each 2" x the width of the fabric; cut 16 sets of 2" Wings from the strips

4 strips, each 4¼" x the width of the fabric; cut 16 sets of 5½" Straight-Grain Kaleidoscopes from the strips

5 squares, each 2½" x 2½"

4 squares, each 4¾" x 4¾"

From the fat quarter, cut:

2½"-wide bias strips as needed for binding

Heart Blocks

1. Referring to "Block Assembly" on pages 16–18, use 3" Kaleidoscopes and 1¼" Wings to make 40 Basic blocks. Trim each block to 2½" x 2½", with the Wing seam at 2⅜" (page 17).

Make 40.

2. Using the Basic blocks and the 2½" light pink squares, lay out 5 Heart blocks. Join the blocks and squares into rows. Press, twisting open the ends of the seams. Join the rows. Press. Mark the midpoint of each edge.

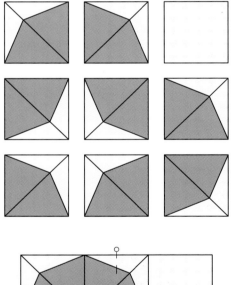

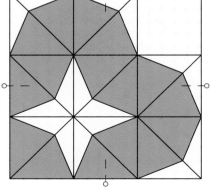

Make 5.

3. Cut each 5½" blue square in half diagonally. Mark the midpoint of each long edge.

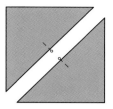

4. With right sides together, sew blue triangles to opposite sides of a Heart block, matching mid-point markings. The triangles will extend beyond the edges of the block. Open out and press the seam allowances toward the triangle.

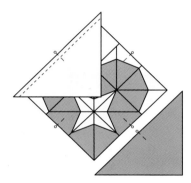

5. Trim the triangle corners even with the edges of the Heart block.

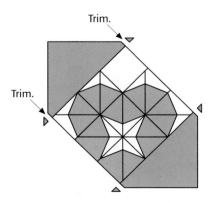

6. Sew blue triangles to the other 2 sides, matching midpoints. Press. Trim to 9" x 9", being careful to leave a ¼" seam allowance at the Heart block points.

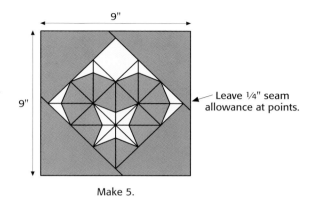

Make 5.

7. Repeat steps 4–6 with the remaining Heart blocks and blue triangles.

Star Blocks

1. Using the remaining Kaleidoscopes and Wings, make 32 Basic blocks. Trim to 4¾" x 4¾", with the Wing seam at 4⅝".

Make 16.   Make 16.

2. Lay out and assemble 4 Star blocks.

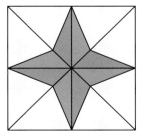

Make 4.

Assembly

Join the Heart blocks and Star blocks into 3 rows of 3 blocks each. Press. Join the rows. Press.

Border

1. Using the blue rectangles, the remaining Basic blocks, and the 4¾" light pink squares, make borders as shown.

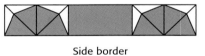

Side border
Make 2.

Top and bottom borders
Make 2.

2. Sew the side borders to the quilt top. Press the seam allowances toward the borders. Add the top and bottom borders. Press.

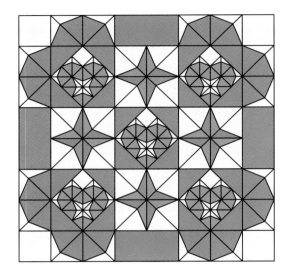

Finishing

Quilting and binding directions begin on page 88.

Hearts and Stars Work Sheet

Border option

PINWHEEL BLOCK PROJECT

If you haven't made the Simply Stellar Sampler, be sure to work through Lessons One and Two (pages 14–18 and 21–24) before making this project. Use scraps and cut and piece just a few of the shapes described. You don't need to cut all the strips and piece all the blocks required for the Sampler.

PINWHEEL STAR QUILT

Quilt size: 40" x 50" (50" x 60" with extra border)
Building block size: 5"
Pinwheel Star size: 10"

Short on time, I limited myself to twelve Pinwheel blocks for this quilt. When I rotated them to create the solid secondary star, I came out with two brown and two green corner pieces. This prompted the two-color border treatment. So you see, I really do design as I go! By contrast, an even number of blocks per row set with a different even number, say 4 x 6, would give you the same fabric in every corner.

An optional border design is included on page 62. Use the Pinwheel Star Work Sheet on page 63 for further exploration or expansion.

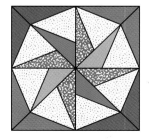

PINWHEEL STAR QUILT by Mary Sue Suit, 1998, Alliance, Nebraska, 40" x 50".

Materials (44"-wide cotton)

½ yd. light green (or ¾ yd.*)

½ yd. green print (or ¾ yd.*)

½ yd. rust (or ¾ yd.*)

½ yd. brown print (or ¾ yd.*)

1 yd. medium green for blocks and border
(or 1½ yds.*)

1 yd. medium brown for blocks and border
(or 1½ yds.*)

1 yd. light spatter print (or 1¼ yds.*)

*With extra border. See instructions on pages 61–62.

Cutting

For instructions on cutting Wing sets, refer to page 15; for Regular Kaleidoscope sets, page 22. Use the 2¼" Wing and 4½" Regular Kaleidoscope templates on page 94, or use Mary Sue's Triangle Ruler.

From the light green, cut:

4 strips, each 2¼" x the width of the fabric

From the green print, cut:

4 strips, each 2¼" x the width of the fabric. With wrong sides up, stack a light green strip on a green print strip. This will make your stars spin clockwise. Cut 30 sets of 2¼" Wings.

From the rust, cut:

4 strips, each 2¼" x the width of the fabric

From the brown print, cut:

4 strips, each 2¼" x the width of the fabric. With wrong sides up, stack a rust print on a brown print strip. Cut 30 sets of 2¼" Wings.

From the medium green, cut:

4 strips, each 2¼" x the width of the fabric

1 strip, 5½" x 20½"

1 strip, 5½" x 30½"

From the medium brown, cut:

4 strips, each 2¼" x the width of the fabric; cut 30 sets of 2¼" Wings

1 strip, 5½" x 20½"

1 strip, 5½" x 30½"

From the light spatter print, cut:

7 strips, each 4½" x the width of the fabric; cut 60 sets of 4½" Regular Kaleidoscopes

Block Assembly

1. Referring to "Block Assembly" on page 22, sew a light green, green print, rust, or brown print Wing to each spatter print Kaleidoscope. Trim the pieced triangles to 5¾". Use a handmade template or Mary Sue's Triangle Ruler.

Trim to 5¾".

2. Referring to the illustration below, lay out the Pinwheel blocks. Sew a medium green or brown Wing to each pieced triangle (page 23). Press, twisting open each end of the seam, then join the pieced units to make Pinwheel blocks. Press. Trim each block to 5½" x 5½", with the wing seam at 5⅜" and the Kaleidoscope point at 5¼".

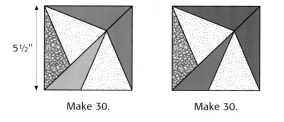

Make 30.   Make 30.

3. Lay out 12 Pinwheel Star blocks. Sew the units together and press.

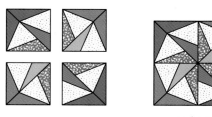

Make 12.

4. Referring to the illustration on the facing page, lay out the quilt center. Sew the blocks into rows. Press. Join the rows. Press.

Border

1. To make the top and bottom borders, sew a Pinwheel block to each end of each 20½"-long strip.

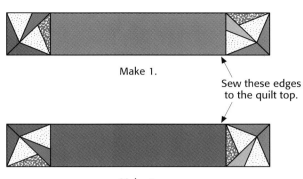

Make 1.

Sew these edges
to the quilt top.

Make 1.

2. To make the side borders, sew 2 Pinwheel blocks to each end of each 30½"-long strip.

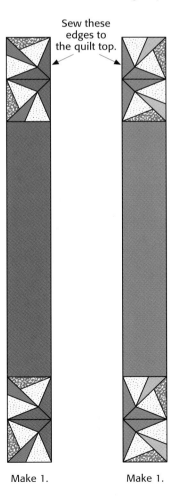

Sew these
edges to
the quilt top.

Make 1.   Make 1.

3. Sew the top and bottom borders to the quilt top. Press the seam allowances toward the borders. Add the side borders. Press the seam allowances toward the borders.

Optional Border

For cutting, use the template sizes and strip widths listed on page 60.

1. With strips stacked wrong sides up, cut 8 light green/green print Wing sets and 8 rust/brown print Wing sets.

2. From the spatter print, cut 16 Regular Kaleidoscope sets.

3. From both the medium green and the medium brown, cut 8 Wing sets; a 5½" x 10½" strip; a 5½" x 20½" strip; and 2 miter sets, each 5½" wide with a miter cut at 5¼" (page 19).

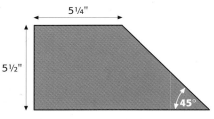

Cut 2 green and 2 brown sets.

4. Make 8 green Pinwheel blocks and 8 brown Pinwheel blocks as described in steps 1–2 on page 60.

5. Referring to the illustration below, sew the pieces together to make border strips. Press.

6. Referring to step 8 on page 87, sew the border strips to the quilt top. Press the seam allowances toward the border.

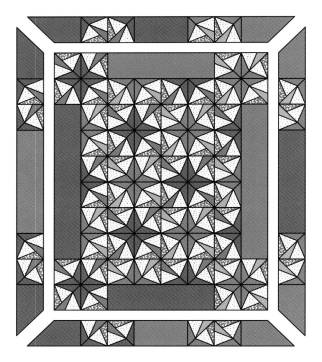

Finishing

Quilting and binding directions begin on page 88. I pieced my binding from leftover fabrics. To do the same, cut 2½"-wide bias strips from scraps.

Pinwheel Star Work Sheet

PIECED DIAMOND BLOCK PROJECT

If you haven't made the Simply Stellar Sampler, be sure to work through Lessons One through Three (pages 14–18 and 21–27) before making the Pieced Diamond block project. Use scraps and cut and piece just a few of the shapes described. You don't need to cut all the strips and piece all the blocks required for the Sampler.

THE CHARMER

Quilt size: 72" x 84"
Building block sizes: 5" and 6"

I used just about every blue and yellow print I had in the house when I made my version of this quilt. Two block sizes provide variety: 5" for the quilt center and 6" for the pieced outer border. To increase the size to 84" x 96", add a plain 6" outer border (fabric not included in the Materials list).

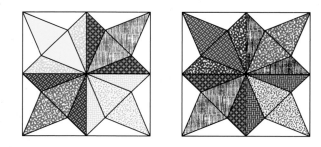

THE CHARMER by Mary Ellen Reynolds, 1998, Alliance, Nebraska, 72" x 84".

Materials (44"-wide cotton)

  5 yds. white for stars, sashing, border, and binding

3¼ yds. *total* assorted blue scraps for stars

1⅞ yds. *total* assorted yellow scraps for stars

  ¼ yd. (or a 5" x 15" scrap) dark blue for sashing squares

NOTE: The cutting directions have been split up to keep the pieces for the 5" and 6" blocks separate.

Cutting for the Quilt Center

For instructions on cutting Wing sets, refer to page 15; for Regular Kaleidoscope sets, page 22. Use the 2¼" Wing and 4½" Regular Kaleidoscope templates on page 94, or use Mary Sue's Triangle Ruler.

From the white, cut:

2 *lengthwise* strips, each 7½" x 64" (side inner borders)

2 *lengthwise* strips, each 7½" x 52" (top and bottom inner borders).

12 *crosswise* strips, each 2¼" x the width of the fabric; cut 48 sets of 2¼" Wings from the strips

17 strips, each 2½" x 10½"

14 rectangles, each 2½" x 5½"

2½"-wide bias strips as needed for binding

From the assorted blues, cut:

2¼"-wide strips; the number of strips you need will depend on the width of your scraps. Cut 32 sets of 2¼" Wings from the strips.

4½"-wide strips; the number of strips you need will depend on the width of your scraps. Cut 32 sets of 4½" Regular Kaleidoscopes from the strips.

From the assorted yellows, cut:

2¼"-wide strips; the number of strips you need will depend on the width of your scraps. Cut 16 sets of 2¼" Wings from the strips.

4½"-wide strips; the number of strips you need will depend on the width of your scraps. Cut 16 sets of 4½" Regular Kaleidoscopes from the strips.

From the dark blue, cut:

12 squares, each 2½" x 2½"

Quilt Center Assembly

1. Lay out the Pieced Diamond blocks as shown. For each block, choose 2 Wings that meet along their short sides (1 white and 1 yellow or blue). Sew these to the Kaleidoscope triangles to make the pieced Kaleidoscopes (page 22). Referring to "Trimming" on pages 25–26, trim the pieced Kaleidoscopes to 5½". Use a handmade template or Mary Sue's Triangle Ruler.

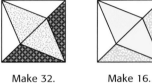

Make 32.   Make 16.

2. Sew the remaining Wings to the pieced units, press, then join the units.

3. Trim each block to 5½" x 5½", with the diamond points at 5¼".

4. Referring to the photo on page 65, lay out the quilt center. Use the 48 blocks completed in step 3, the white sashing strips, and the blue sashing squares. To duplicate the look of the photo quilt, place 8 yellow blocks in the middle and have the remaining yellow blocks run diagonally to the corners.

5. Join Pieced Diamond blocks to make Pieced Diamond Star Variation blocks as shown. Sew the remaining blue blocks into pairs.

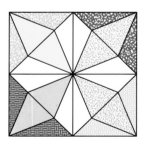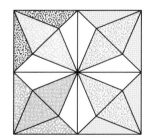

Make 4.   Make 2.

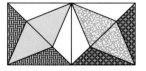

Make 10.

6. Sew the blocks and vertical sashing strips into rows. Press. Sew the horizontal sashing strips and the sashing squares into rows. Press. Join the rows. Press.

Inner Border

1. Measure your quilt top. If it does not measure 36½" x 48½", refer to "Adding Borders" on page 87 to calculate one-half the finished size.

2. Fold the 7½"-wide border strips in half crosswise. On the top and bottom borders, measure 18" (or your width result from step 1) from the fold, mark, and cut a 45-degree angle. On the side borders, measure 24" (or your length result from step 1) from the fold, mark, and cut a 45-degree angle (page 87).

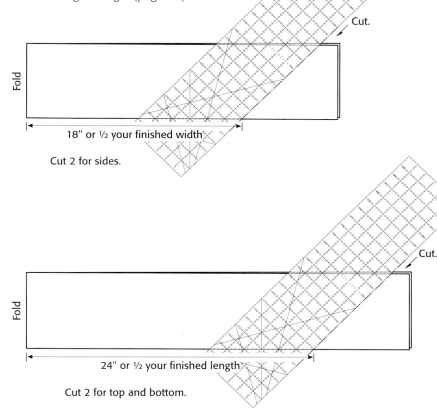

Cut 2 for sides.

18" or ½ your finished width

Fold

24" or ½ your finished length

Cut 2 for top and bottom.

3. Referring to step 8 on page 87, sew the border strips to the quilt center. Press the seam allowances toward the border.

4. Trim the quilt top to exactly 48½" x 60½".

Cutting for the Pieced Outer Border

Use the 2½" Wing and 5" Regular Kaleidoscope templates on page 95, or use Mary Sue's Triangle Ruler.

From the white, cut:

2½"-wide strips; the number of strips you need will depend on the width of your scraps. Cut 88 sets of 2½" Wings from the strips.

From the blue, cut:

2½"-wide strips; the number of strips you need will depend on the width of your scraps. Cut 56 sets of 2½" Wings from the strips.

5¼"-wide strips; the number of strips you need will depend on the width of your scraps. Cut 56 sets of 5" Regular Kaleidoscopes from the strips.

From the yellow, cut

2½"-wide strips; the number of strips you need will depend on the width of your scraps. Cut 32 sets of 2½" Wings from the strips.

5¼"-wide strips; the number of strips you need will depend on the width of your scraps. Cut 32 sets of 5" Regular Kaleidoscopes from the strips.

Assembling the Pieced Outer Border

1. Lay out the Pieced Diamond blocks as shown. Assemble the blocks, following steps 1–3 on page 66. Trim the pieced Kaleidoscopes to 6¾". Trim the blocks to 6½" x 6½", with the diamond point at 6¼" (pages 25–26).

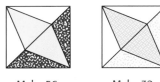

Make 56.   Make 32.

2. Join the blocks to make 22 Pieced Diamond Star Variation blocks.

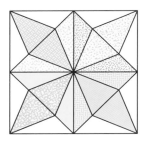 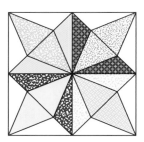

Make 4.   Make 8.

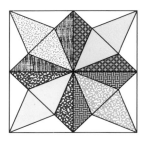

Make 10.

3. Assemble the borders as shown. Press.

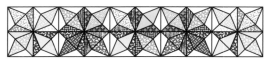

Side border
Make 2.

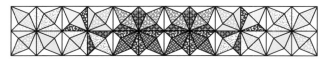

Top and bottom borders
Make 2.

4. Lay the borders along the edges of the quilt top. Referring to the illustration below, check that the yellow diamonds in the yellow/blue stars are oriented properly. Sew the side borders to the quilt top. Press the seam allowances toward the border. Sew the top and bottom borders to the quilt top. Press the seam allowances toward the border.

Finishing

Quilting and binding directions begin on page 88.

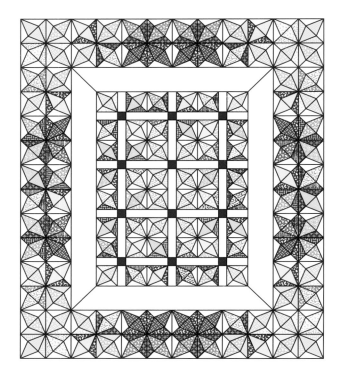

Pieced Diamond Work Sheet

Look for interlocking patterns. Copy and cut apart to explore endless options.

COMBINATION PROJECTS

Before making any of the combination projects, be sure to complete Lessons One through Three (pages 14–18 and 21–27) of the Simply Stellar Sampler. Use scraps and cut and piece just a few of the shapes described. You don't need to cut all the strips and piece all the blocks required for the Sampler.

CHRISTMAS WREATH

Quilt size: 24" x 24"
Building block size: 3"

This holiday wall hanging has a hidden advantage. You can disguise mistakes by placing buttons, bows, or fabric yo-yos in strategic places.

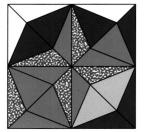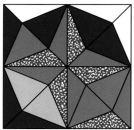

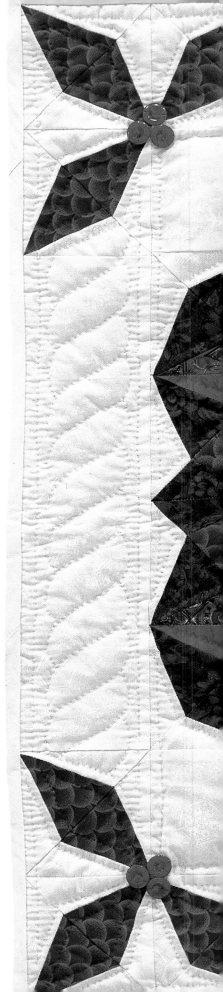

CHRISTMAS WREATH by Mary Sue Suit, 1998, Alliance, Nebraska, 24" x 24".

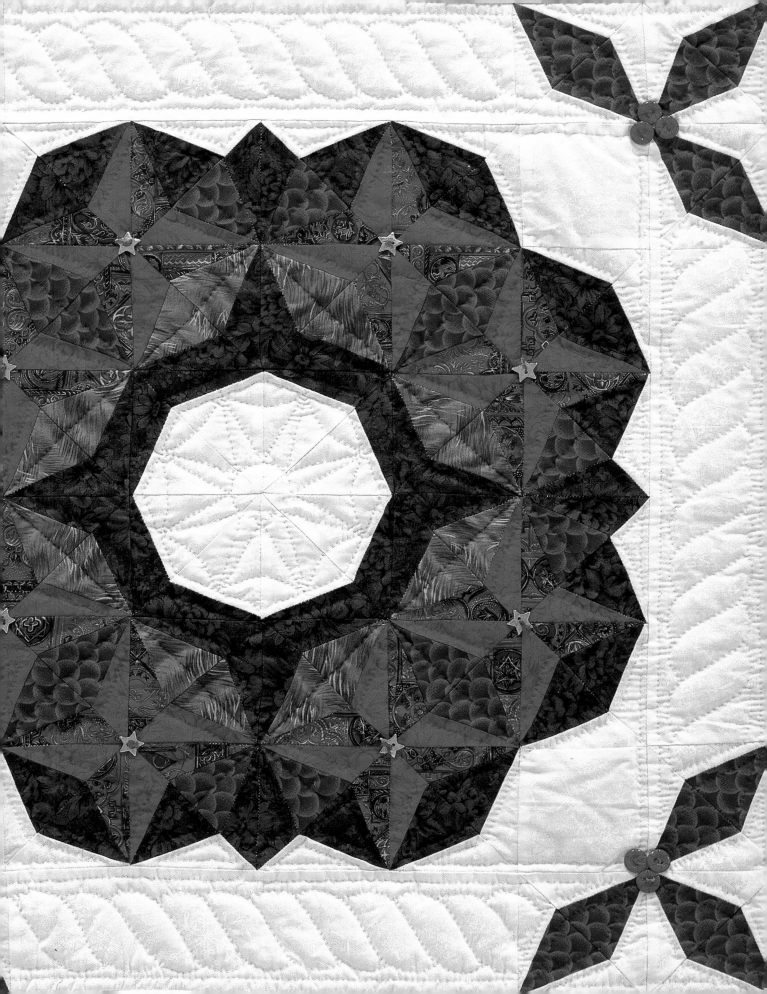

Materials (44"-wide cotton)

⅜ yd.   dark green
¼ yd.   red tone-on-tone
¼ yd.   red print
⅛ yd.   light green
¼ yd.   medium green
1 yd.   white for background, borders, and binding
12   buttons, yo-yos, or beads for holly berries
8   star buttons for star centers

Cutting

For instructions on cutting Wing sets, refer to page 15; for Regular Kaleidoscope sets, page 22; for Straight-Grain Kaleidoscope sets, page 16. Use the 1½" Wing, 3" Regular Kaleidoscope, and 4" Straight-Grain Kaleidoscope templates on page 91, or use Mary Sue's Triangle Ruler.

From the dark green, cut:

3 strips, each 1½" x the width of the fabric; cut 16 sets of 1½" Wings from the strips

1 strip, 3" x the width of the fabric; cut 12 sets of 3" Regular Kaleidoscopes from the strip

From the red tone-on-tone, cut:

3 strips, each 1½" x the width of the fabric

From the red print, cut:

3 strips, each 1½" x the width of the fabric; place the red tone-on-tone and the red print strips right sides together. Always stack the strips with the red print on top. Cut 32 sets of 1½" Wings from the strips.

From the light green, cut:

1 strip, 3" x the width of the fabric; cut 8 sets of 3" Regular Kaleidoscopes from the strip

From the medium green, cut:

2 strips, each 3" x the width of the fabric; cut 20 sets of 3" Regular Kaleidoscopes from the strips

From the white, cut:

6 strips, each 1½" x the width of the fabric; cut 36 sets of 1½" Wings from the strips

1 strip, 3" x the width of the fabric; cut 4 sets of 3¾" Straight-Grain Kaleidoscopes from the strip

4 squares, each 3½" x 3½"

4 strips, each 3½" x 12½", for borders

2½"-wide bias strips as needed for binding

Block Assembly

1. Using the white Straight-Grain Kaleidoscope sets and 4 dark green Wing sets, make 4 Basic blocks. Trim each block to 3½" x 3½", with the Wing seam at 3⅜" (page 18).

Make 4.

2. Lay out the Pieced Diamond blocks as shown. For each block, choose 2 Wings that meet along their short sides. Sew these to Kaleidoscope triangles to make pieced Kaleidoscopes (page 23). Referring to "Block Assembly" on page 23, trim the pieced Kaleidoscopes to 3¾". Use a handmade template (page 96) or Mary Sue's Triangle Ruler.

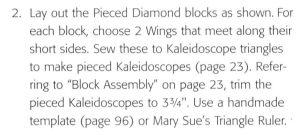

Make 8.   Make 4.   Make 8.

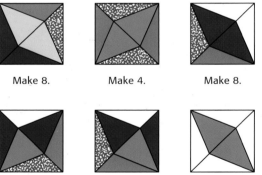

Make 4.   Make 4.   Make 12.

3. Sew the remaining Wings to the pieced units, press, then join the units.

4. Trim each block to 3½" x 3½", with the diamond points at 3¼" (pages 25–26). You should have a total of 40 blocks. Set the 12 medium green/white blocks aside.

5. Referring to the photo on page 71, use the 28 remaining Pieced Diamond blocks, the Basic blocks from step 1, and the 3½" white squares to lay out the quilt center. Sew the blocks into rows. Press. Join the rows. Press.

Holly Border

1. Sew a medium green Pieced Diamond block to each end of each white border strip as shown. Press the seam allowances toward the white border strip.

Make 4.

2. Referring to the photo on page 71, sew 2 of the units from step 1 to the sides of the quilt center. Press the seam allowances toward the border.

3. To make the top and bottom borders, sew a Pieced Diamond block to each end of the 2 remaining units from step 1 as shown. Press.

Make 2.

4. Sew the units from step 3 to the top and bottom of the quilt center. Press the seam allowances toward the border.

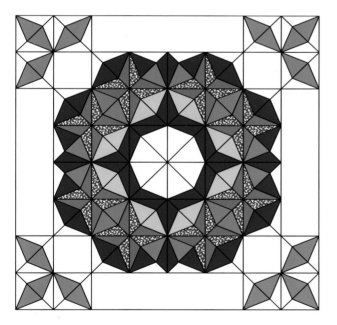

Finishing

1. Quilt as desired.

2. Sew buttons, yo-yos, or beads in the corners for holly berries. If desired, add star buttons at the centers of the red stars.

3. Bind the edges (page 89).

WHAT IF by Mary Sue Suit, 1998, Alliance, Nebraska, 40" x 40". This is the quilt that inspired me to make Christmas Wreath. It shows the wonderful design possibilities of the Pieced Diamond block.

TO A WILD ROSE

Quilt size: 27" x 27"
Block size: 3"

To a Wild Rose combines elements of Basic, Pinwheel, and Pieced Diamond blocks for wonderful design possibilities. The piecing is intricate, so pay close attention to the trimming directions.

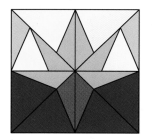

TO A WILD ROSE by Mary Sue Suit, 1998, Alliance, Nebraska, 27" x 27".

Materials (44"-wide cotton)

2 strips *each* of yellow and light pink, each
        1½" x at least 40"

1 medium pink strip, 3" x at least 40"

½ yd. dark teal for roses and binding

⅜ yd. maroon

⅝ yd. light teal for background and outer border

¾ yd. light floral print for background

Cutting

For instructions on cutting Wing sets, refer to page 15; for Regular Kaleidoscope sets, page 22; for Straight-Grain Kaleidoscope sets, pages 15–16. Use the 1½" Wing, 3" Regular Kaleidoscope, and 4" Straight-Grain templates on page 91, or use Mary Sue's Triangle Ruler.

NOTE: When cutting, place all fabrics same sides together—even for the Pinwheel blocks.

From the yellow strips, cut:

12 sets of 1½" Wings

From the light pink strips, cut:

12 sets of 1½" Wings

From the medium pink strip, cut:

4 sets of 4" Straight-Grain Kaleidoscopes

From the dark teal, cut:

2 strips, each 1½" x the width of the fabric; cut 8 sets of 1½" Wings from the strips

2½"-wide bias strips as needed for binding

From the maroon, cut:

3 strips, each 1½" x the width of the fabric; cut 16 sets of 1½" Wings from the strips

1 strip, 3" x the width of the fabric; cut 8 sets of 4" Straight-Grain Kaleidoscopes from the strip

From the light teal, cut:

3 strips, each 1½" x the width of the fabric; cut 16 sets of 1½" Wings from the strips

1 strip, 3" x the width of the fabric; cut 4 sets of 3" Regular Kaleidoscopes from the strip

4 strips, each 2" x 30", for outer border

From the floral print, cut:

3 strips, each 3" x the width of the fabric; cut 16 sets of 3" Regular Kaleidoscopes and 12 sets of 4" Straight-Grain Kaleidoscopes from the strips

2 strips, each 3½" x the width of the fabric, for miter corners

Block Assembly

1. Referring to "Block Assembly" on pages 16–17, assemble the blocks shown below. Trim the blocks to 3½", with the Wing seam at 3⅜" (page 17).

    Make 4.   Make 4.

    Make 4.   Make 8.

2. Lay out the blocks shown below. Referring to "Block Assembly" on pages 22–23, assemble the blocks. Sew the Pinwheel Wings to the Kaleidoscope triangles first to form the pieced Kaleidoscope units. Press. Referring to page 23, trim the pieced Kaleidoscopes to 3¾". Use a handmade template (page 96) or Mary Sue's Triangle Ruler. Trim the blocks to 3½", with the Wing seam at 3⅜" (pages 2–24).

Left Pinwheel   Right Pinwheel
   Make 4.   Make 4.

3. Lay out the blocks shown below. Sew the dark teal or maroon Wings to the Kaleidoscope triangles first. Press.

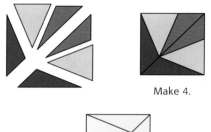

Make 4.

Make 4.

4. Trim the pieced Kaleidoscopes to 3¾" as described on pages 25–26. Add the remaining Wings, press, and join the halves. Press. Trim the block to 3½" as you would a Basic block (page 17).

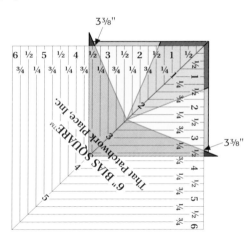

5. The Open Pinwheel block is made up of one-half of a Basic block and one-half of a Pinwheel block. Lay out 8 Open Pinwheel blocks, 4 left and 4 right. Place the straight grain of the Kaleidoscope triangles at the edges.

Left Open Pinwheel   Right Open Pinwheel

6. For the Basic block half, sew the pink Wing to the 3¾" floral Straight-Grain Kaleidoscope triangle. Press the seam allowances toward the darker fabric.

Make 4.   Make 4.

7. For the Pinwheel half, sew the pink Wing to the floral Regular Kaleidoscope. Press. Trim to 3¾" as described on pages 25–26. Add the light teal Wing. Press.

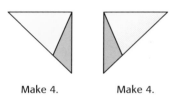

Make 4.   Make 4.

8. Lay out the 2 halves to form a block. Sew the halves together. Press. Repeat with the remaining half-blocks to make 4 left Open Pinwheels and 4 right Open Pinwheels. Trim the Open Pinwheel blocks to 3½" x 3½", with the Wing seams at 3⅜".

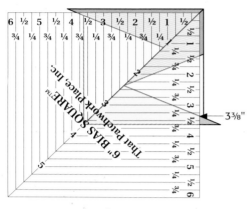

Left

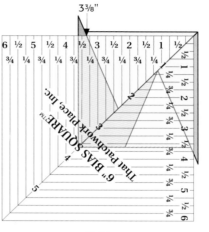

Right

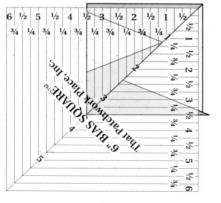

Left

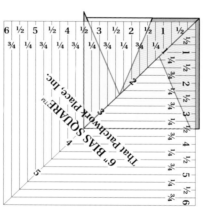

Right

9. Referring to the illustration on the facing page, lay out the center of the quilt top. Sew the blocks into rows. Press. Join the rows. Press.

Pieced Border

1. Lay the 3½"-wide floral strips right sides together and remove the selvages. At the bottom of the strip, measure 6¼" from the left-hand edge and mark. At the mark, cut a 45-degree angle. From the diagonal cut, measure 6¼" along the top of the strip, mark, and cut straight across the strip as shown. Repeat to cut a total of 4 miter pairs.

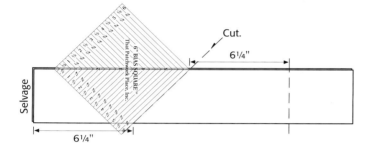

2. Using the remaining Basic blocks and the floral miter sets, lay out the borders as shown. Stitch and press.

3. Referring to step 8 on page 87, sew the border strips to the quilt top. Press the seam allowances toward the border.

Outer Border

1. Measure your quilt top. If it does not measure 24½" x 24½", refer to "Adding Borders" on page 87 to calculate one-half the finished size.

2. Fold the light teal border strips in half crosswise. Measure 12" (or your result from step 1) from the fold, mark, and cut a 45-degree angle (page 87).

3. Sew the border strips to the quilt top. Press the seam allowances toward the border.

Finishing

Quilting and binding directions begin on page 88.

SPRING POSIES

Quilt size: 60" x 70"
Building block size: 5"
Spring Posy block size: 10"

I've found that a white woven bedspread makes the perfect backdrop for a "comfort size" quilt on a king-size bed. It looks great and gives Snooks, my old English sheep dog, something washable to lie against at the foot of the bed.

You can customize the Spring Posies design in several ways. You can stop after the first mitered-corner row for a dainty 30" x 40" wall hanging. Or, you can enlarge the building blocks to 6" for a quilt that would measure 96" x 108" with an extra row of Rosebud blocks.

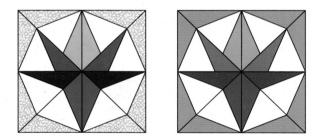

SPRING POSIES by Mary Sue Suit, 1998, Alliance, Nebraska, 60" x 70".
It's amazing that straight-line piecing can produce so many graceful curves!

Materials (44"-wide cotton)

½ yd.   green for posies and binding
⅞ yd.   white for background
1½ yds. pink floral
¼ yd.   light purple
¼ yd.   medium purple
⅝ yd.   dark purple for posies and outer border
⅜ yd.   medium mauve
⅜ yd.   medium-dark mauve
1½ yds. maroon for posies and outer border
1¼ yds. light print for background
1¼ yds. mauve for background

Cutting

For instructions on cutting Wing sets, refer to page 15; for Regular Kaleidoscope sets, page 22; for Straight-Grain Kaleidoscope sets, pages 15–16. Use the 2¼" Wing, 4½" Regular Kaleidoscope, and 5¾" Straight-Grain Kaleidoscope templates on page 94, or use Mary Sue's Triangle Ruler.

NOTE: When cutting, place all fabrics same sides together—even for the Pinwheel blocks.

From the green, cut:

4 strips, each 2¼" x the width of the fabric; cut 18 sets of 2¼" Wings from the strips

2½"-wide bias strips as needed for binding

From the white, cut:

2 strips, each 4½" x the width of the fabric; cut 18 sets of 4½" Regular Kaleidoscopes from the strips

4 strips, each 4½" x the width of the fabric; cut 18 sets of 5¾" Straight-Grain Kaleidoscopes from the strips

From the pink floral, cut:

11 strips, each 2¼" x the width of the fabric; cut 54 sets of 2¼" Wings from the strips

2 strips, each 5½" x the width of the fabric, for miter pairs

From the light purple, cut:

2 strips, each 2¼" x the width of the fabric; cut 8 sets of 2¼" Wings from the strips

From the medium purple, cut:

2 strips, each 2¼" x the width of the fabric; cut 8 sets of 2¼" Wings from the strips

From the dark purple, cut:

2 strips, each 2¼" x the width of the fabric; cut 10 sets of 2¼" Wings from the strips

2 strips, each 5½" x the width of the fabric, for border

From the medium mauve, cut:

2 strips, each 2¼" x the width of the fabric; cut 10 sets of 2¼" Wings from the strips

From the medium-dark mauve, cut:

2 strips, each 2¼" x the width of the fabric; cut 10 sets of 2¼" Wings from the strips

From the maroon, cut:

4 *lengthwise* strips, each 5½" x 45", for border

6 strips, each 2¼" x the width of the fabric; cut 12 sets of 2¼" Wings from the strips

From the light print, cut:

7 strips, each 4½" x the width of the fabric; cut 60 sets of 4½" Regular Kaleidoscopes from the strips

From the mauve for the background, cut:

9 strips, each 2¼" x the width of the fabric; cut 44 sets of 2¼" Wings from the strips

2 rectangles, each 5½" x 10½"

2 rectangles, each 5½" x 20½"

Block Assembly

In the following blocks, trim pieced Kaleidoscopes to 5½" or 5¾", using handmade templates (page 96), or Mary Sue's Triangle Ruler.

1. Lay out Pieced Diamond blocks as shown. For each block, choose 2 Wings that meet along their short sides. Sew these to Kaleidoscope triangles to make pieced Kaleidoscopes (page 22). Press, then trim to 5½" as described on page 25. Sew the remaining Wings to the pieced units, press, then join the units. Trim each block to 5½" x 5½", with the diamond points at 5¼" (pages 25–26).

Make 2.   Make 2.   Make 12.

 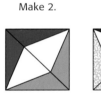

Make 2.   Make 2.   Make 2.   Make 2.

Make 8.   Make 8.   Make 4.   Make 4.

2. Lay out Open Pinwheel blocks as shown, placing the straight grain of the Kaleidoscope triangles at the edge of the block. The Open Pinwheel is made up of half of a Basic block and half of a Pinwheel block. Refer to steps 5–8 on pages 77–78. Trim the pieced Kaleidoscope in the Pinwheel half to 5¾". Trim the block to 5½", with the Wing seam at 5⅜".

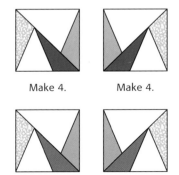

Make 4.   Make 4.

Make 2.   Make 2.

3. Lay out 12 pink floral/white Basic blocks as shown. Referring to "Block Assembly" on page 17, assemble the blocks. Trim the blocks to 5½", with the Wing seams at 5⅜".

Make 12.

4. Lay out Pinwheel blocks as shown. Referring to "Block Assembly" on pages 23–24, assemble the block. Sew the Pinwheel Wings to the Kaleidoscope triangles first. Trim the pieced Kaleidoscope to 5¾". Trim the blocks to 5½", with the Wing seams at 5⅜".

Make 8.   Make 8.

Make 4.   Make 4.

5. Lay out the middle of the quilt as shown. Sew the blocks into rows. Press. Join the rows. Press the quilt top.

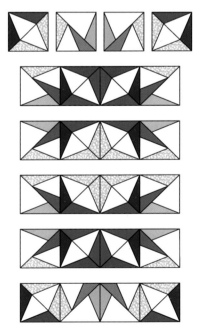

6. Sew the 12 pink floral/white Basic blocks into units as shown. Press.

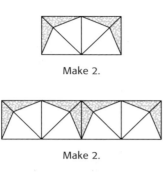

Make 2.

Make 2.

7. Cut the 5½"-wide pink floral strips in half crosswise. Measure 5¼" from the left edge along the bottom; mark and cut a 45-degree angle. Measure 5¼" from this cut along the top edge and cut straight across the strips. Make 4 miter pairs.

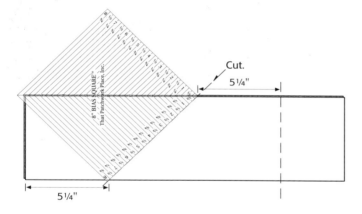

Cut.

5¼"

8" BIAS SQUARE™
That Patchwork Place, Inc.

5¼"

8. Sew the miter pairs to the units from step 6. Press.

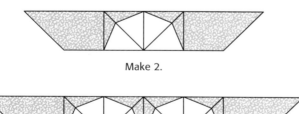

Make 2.

Make 2.

9. Referring to step 8 on page 87, sew the pieced units to the middle section.

Posy Border

1. Use the remaining building blocks to make maroon and purple Posy blocks.

Make 8.   Make 4.

2. Join the pink floral/light print/mauve Pieced Diamond blocks and the mauve rectangles as shown. Press.

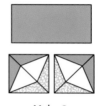

Make 2.

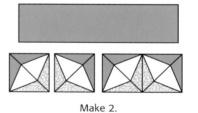

Make 2.

3. Sew the maroon and purple Posy blocks to the units from step 2 to make the pieced borders. Press.

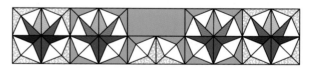

Make 2.

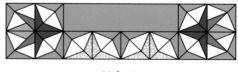

Make 2.

4. Sew the side borders to the middle section. Press the seam allowances toward the border. Add the top and bottom borders. Press the seam allowances toward the border.

Outer Border

1. Place the 5½"-wide dark purple strips right sides together and cut 4 purple miter pairs as shown.

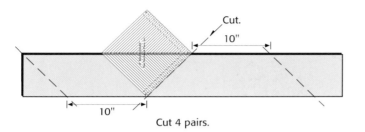

Cut.

10"

10"

Cut 4 pairs.

2. Fold each 5½"-wide maroon strip in half crosswise and cut miter pairs as shown.

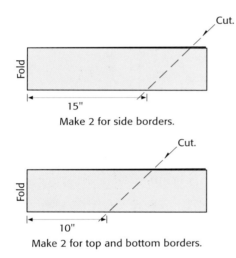

Cut.

Fold

15"

Make 2 for side borders.

Cut.

Fold

10"

Make 2 for top and bottom borders.

3. Sew 2 purple border strips to each maroon border strip. Press.

Make 2 short and 2 long.

4. Sew the pieced borders to the quilt top (page 87). Press the seam allowances toward the border.

Finishing

Quilting and binding directions begin on page 88.

Spring Posies Work Sheet

Optional Border A

Optional Border B

TECHNIQUES FOR FINISHING

Adding Borders

You may have noticed that all of the borders in this book are mitered. I don't know why people are so afraid of miters—they're really quite simple. One benefit of mitering is that it can take your quilt from beginning to advanced in appearance.

1. Measure your quilt top from side to side, across its center, to determine its width.

2. Subtract ½" from this measurement for seam allowances. This is the finished width dimension.

3. Divide your result from step 2 in half.
   (Working through steps 1–3, if your top measured 25¼" across, you would subtract ½" for seam allowances to get the finished dimension: 24¾". You would then divide this number in half: 24¾" ÷ 2 = 12⅜".)

4. Fold your top border strip in half crosswise, with the fold at left.

5. Measure at the bottom edge of the strip, using the number you got in step 3 (one-half the finished width). Mark.

6. Position a square ruler with the diagonal line along the top edge of the border strip and the ruler to the left of and just hitting your mark. Cut along the ruler's edge.

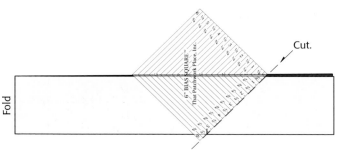

7. Repeat steps 1–6 for the side borders, measuring the *length* of your quilt top in step 1.

8. Stitch the border strips to the quilt top in the order shown, referring to "Block Assembly" on pages 20–21 for specific stitching instructions.

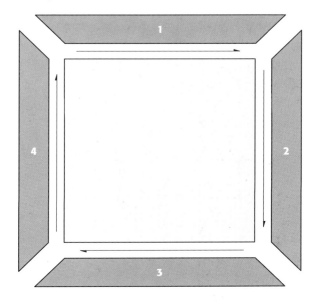

Preparing and Marking

Now that you have a beautiful quilt top, it is important to remember that it isn't a quilt until it's quilted! No matter how perfect the colors and piecing are, it won't be an heirloom quilt until it's finished.

After much trial and error, I learned that before I even think about assembling the layers, I need to give the quilt top one last press and check the back for any long threads that need to be trimmed. I also make sure no dark threads are long enough to show through a lighter section.

Most quilters mark the quilting pattern on the quilt top before basting the layers together. This is especially important if you quilt on a frame or with a group. I prefer to quilt on a hoop and mark as I go. I usually outline quilt ¼" from the seam. If several pieces form one design element, as in the large petals of the Wild Rose block, I outline the entire design element rather than each piece. Then I often quilt something within the element.

I like to use stencils. There are so many on the market, I always find something that works. I have used continuous-line machine-quilting stencils with great success. I am sure you noticed that there are a lot of unpieced outer borders in this book. These are great places for quilting. I like to fill borders with graceful cables or curved lines to contrast the straight lines of the piecing.

If the fabric is light enough, I prefer a very sharp, hard lead pencil for marking. Mark as lightly as possible. Water-soluble quilt-marking pens are available, but I have had difficulty removing the marks, and quite often, the one pen I have has dried out. When you live in the "outback," you can't always run out to buy a new pen when you need it.

Pink, yellow, and white pencils work well for marking dark fabrics. Because I usually mark as I go, I often use soap slivers to mark dark fabrics. Save the little pieces of soap that haunt the bathroom and let them dry out. They work best if they are thin and hard. Avoid using moisturizing bars, as they may be oily. Soap helps the needle slide through the fabric and has usually disappeared by the time you have finished the quilting. If not, wipe off the soap with a damp cloth.

I use ¼"-wide masking tape, available in quilt shops and catalogs, to mark straight lines. Rather than taping the entire top at once, position the tape as you quilt. You can usually use one piece of tape several times before discarding it. Be aware that the tape can be difficult to remove when left in place too long, and it may leave a residue.

Whether you mark your quilt top before or after you baste the layers together, be sure that you *do* baste. This is another step I grew into the hard way. If you quilt in a hoop rather than a frame, it is doubly important to baste the quilt "sandwich" generously.

To baste your quilt:

Lay the backing fabric, wrong side up, on a flat surface. I use the living-room floor. Smooth out all the wrinkles. I allow extra backing fabric when hoop quilting, at least 2" on each side.

Spread the batting on top of the backing, making sure it lies flat. You may want to let the batting "breathe," or relax, before basting.

Lay the pressed quilt top, right side up, on top of the other two layers. Smooth out any wrinkles, making sure all three layers lie flat.

Using light thread and long basting stitches, baste

from the center of the quilt to each corner. Fill in the remaining areas with basting rows spaced 4" to 6" apart.

Because I quilt on a hoop, the quilt sandwich gets manhandled quite a bit. To protect the edges of the top and batting, I bring the excess backing around to the front and baste it in place. This keeps the quilt top's edges from fraying and the batting from stretching as I quilt.

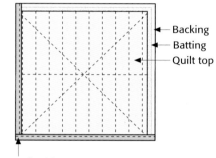

Fold excess backing
to front and baste.

Quilting

Once basted, the quilt sandwich is ready for quilting. Quilting is the best part of the process for me. It wasn't always so, but I now think there can never be too much quilting on a project. Don't be discouraged if your first stitches seem a little long. If you start quilting in the middle of the quilt, by the time you reach the edges they will be much smaller. For hand-quilting instructions, I recommend *Loving Stitches* by Jeana Kimball, or you can take a hand-quilting class.

My favorite trick is using a rubber (or banker's) finger on my right index finger. I injured my finger at one point and could not exert enough pressure on the needle to pull it through the fabric. Wearing the finger nubby side in allows me to quilt longer with less fatigue. It can be cumbersome to start with and it does get a little warm, but both problems are of little consequence when not quilting at all is the alternative.

Binding

When the quilting is complete, add the binding. The binding can be cut on the straight of grain or on the bias. I prefer bias binding because it wears better. As a rule, allow ½ yard of fabric to bind a crib or wall-size quilt, ¾ yard for twin, 1 yard for double or queen, and 1¼ yards for king.

To bind your quilt:

Cut the binding fabric into 2½"-wide bias strips.

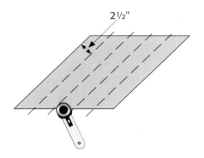

Sew the bias strips together end to end to make one long bias strip. Press the seams open.

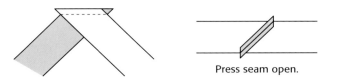

Press seam open.

Fold the strip in half lengthwise, wrong sides together, and press.

Fold line

I include a step most others feel is unnecessary. I do not know if it is just me, or my machine, but I often find pulls and ripples between the last quilted row and the binding. To prevent this, baste through all three layers at the outer edges of the quilt top, making sure everything is flat and smooth. Then trim the excess batting and backing.

Unfold one end of the binding and turn it under ¼". Starting in the center on one side of the quilt, stitch the binding to the quilt with the raw edges of the binding even with the edges of the quilt top. I use a ⅜"-wide seam allowance. Stitch to within ⅜" of the corner. Backstitch and remove the quilt from the machine. Turn the top so you are ready to stitch the next side. To miter the corner, fold the binding up as shown to form a 45-degree angle.

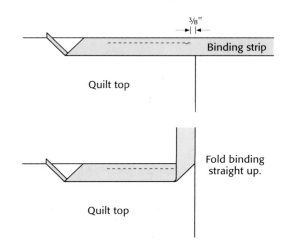

Binding strip

Quilt top

Fold binding straight up.

Quilt top

Fold the binding down, keeping the fold even with the top edge of the quilt and the raw edges of the binding even with the side edge of the quilt. Pin the pleat formed at the fold in place. Stitch, ending the stitching ⅜" from the next corner. Repeat the process for the remaining sides.

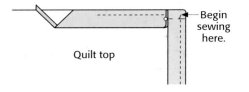

Begin sewing here.

Quilt top

When you reach the beginning of the binding, cut the binding 1" longer than needed and tuck the end inside the beginning of the strip. Fold the binding over the raw edges of the quilt and blindstitch in place on the quilt back. The corners will automatically form miters as you turn them. Slipstitch the miters closed.

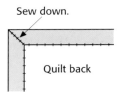

Sew down.

Quilt back

MEET THE AUTHOR

Mary Sue Suit lives with her family—one husband, two kids, one dog, and a station wagon—in western Nebraska. A self-taught quilter, Mary Sue is always looking for the quickest way to do things. Her work has been included in shows at the Castle Art Gallery and the Yellowstone Exhibition. She is an active member of the Panhandle Quilt Guild, and she writes a monthly column for *The Baldwin City Ledger*. Mary Sue's book *All the Blocks Are Geese* is also a That Patchwork Place publication.

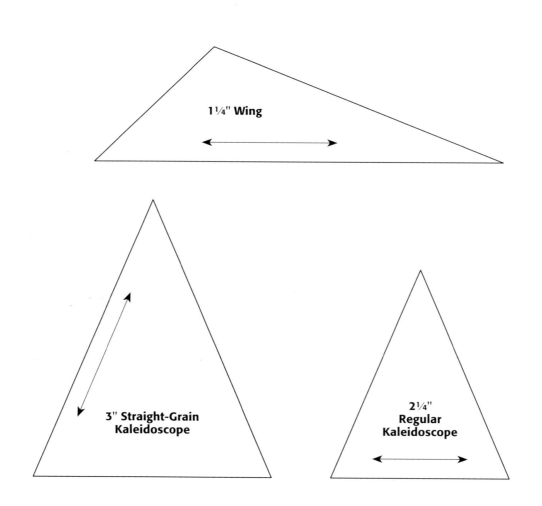

1¼" **Wing**

3" **Straight-Grain Kaleidoscope**

2¼" **Regular Kaleidoscope**

2" Block Templates

Wing strip: 1¼"
 8 Wing sets per strip set
Kaleidoscope strip: 2¼"
 19 Regular Kaleidoscope sets per strip set
 11 Straight-Grain Kaleidoscope sets per strip set

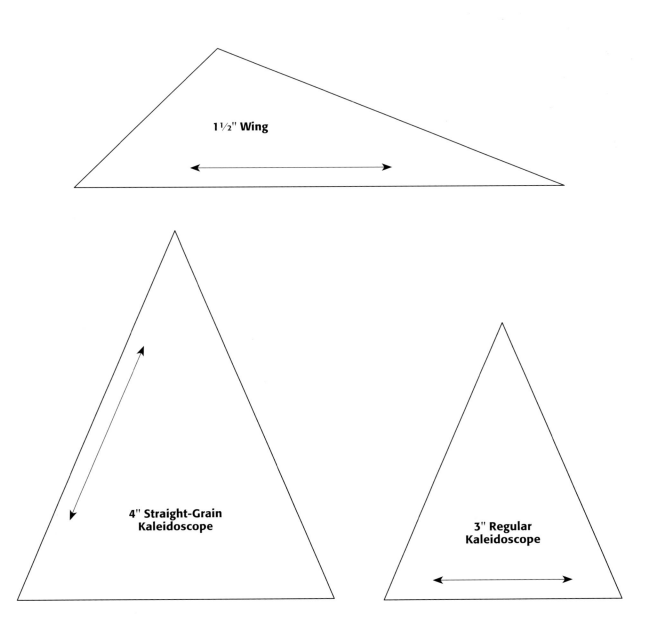

1½" Wing

4" Straight-Grain Kaleidoscope

3" Regular Kaleidoscope

3" Block Templates

Wing strip: 1½"
  6 Wing sets per strip set
Kaleidoscope strip: 3"
  15 Regular Kaleidoscope sets per strip set
  8 Straight-Grain Kaleidoscope sets per strip set

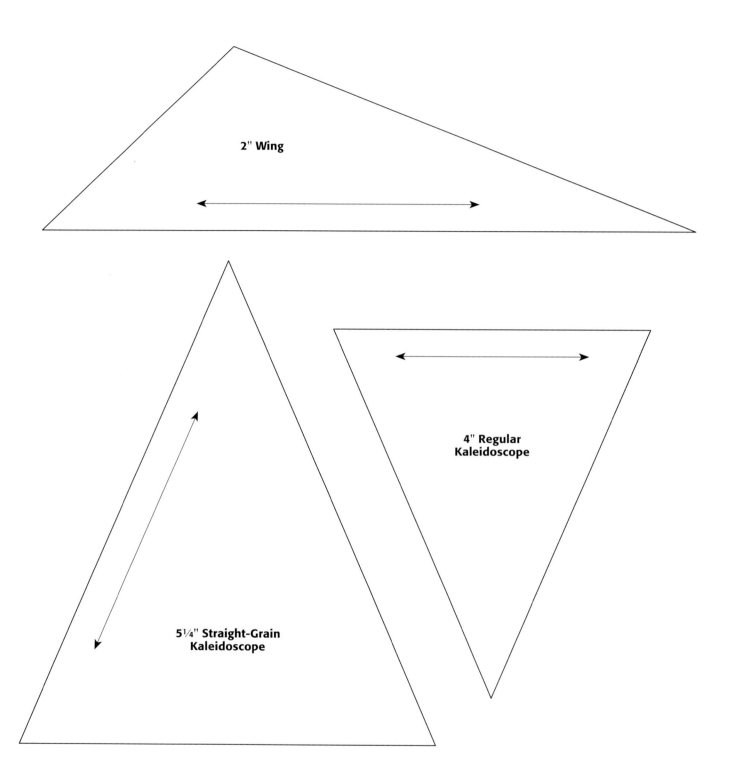

2" Wing

5¼" Straight-Grain Kaleidoscope

4" Regular Kaleidoscope

4" Block Templates

Wing strip: 2"
  5 Wing sets per strip set
Kaleidoscope strip: 4"
  11 Regular Kaleidoscope sets per strip set
  6 Straight-Grain Kaleidoscope sets per strip set

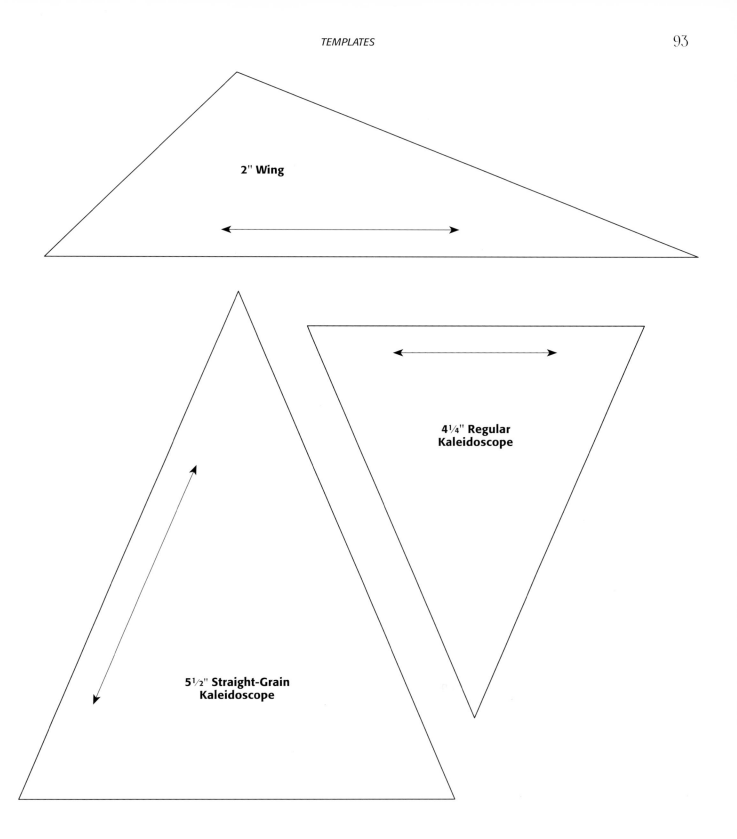

2" Wing

4¼" Regular Kaleidoscope

5½" Straight-Grain Kaleidoscope

4¼" Block Templates

Wing strip: 2"
   5 Wing sets per strip set
Kaleidoscope strip: 4¼"
   10 Regular Kaleidoscope sets per strip set
   5 Straight-Grain Kaleidoscope sets per strip set

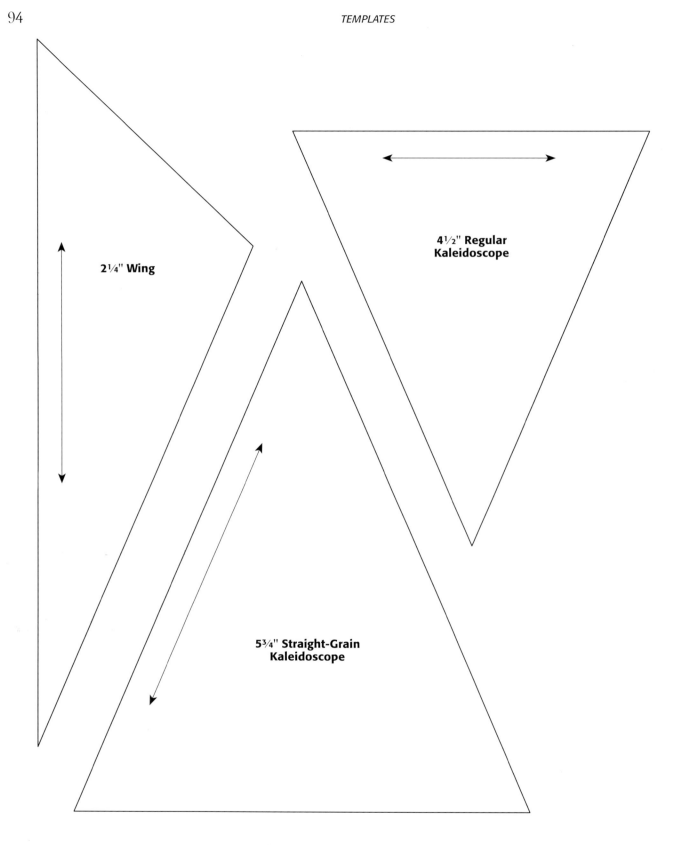

2¼" Wing

4½" Regular Kaleidoscope

5¾" Straight-Grain Kaleidoscope

5" Block Templates

Wing strip: 2¼"
  5 Wing sets per strip set
Kaleidoscope strip: 4½"
   9 Regular Kaleidoscope sets per strip set
   5 Straight-Grain Kaleidoscope sets per strip set

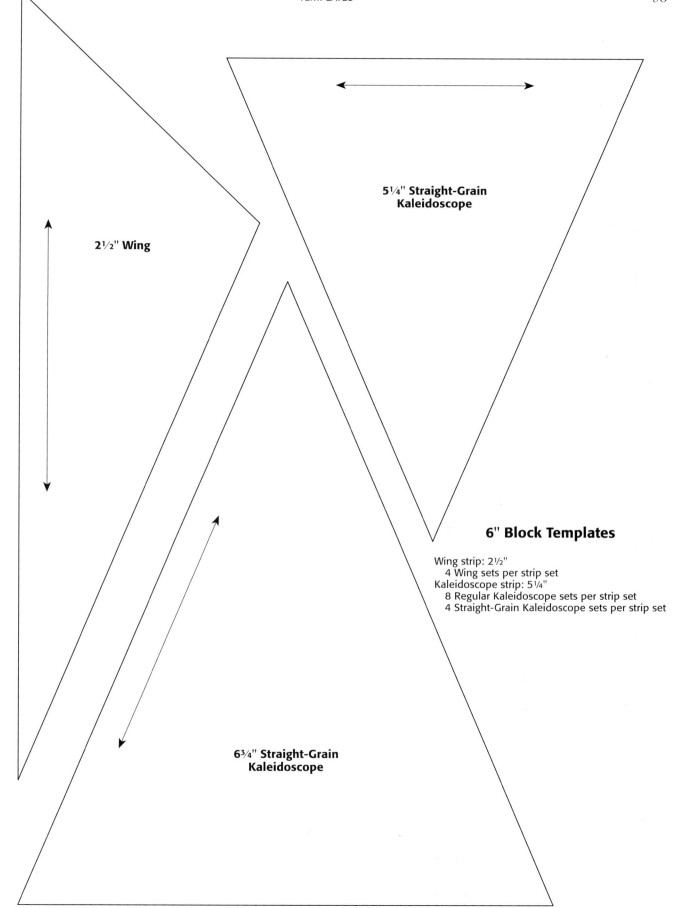

2½" Wing

5¼" Straight-Grain Kaleidoscope

6" Block Templates

Wing strip: 2½"
   4 Wing sets per strip set
Kaleidoscope strip: 5¼"
   8 Regular Kaleidoscope sets per strip set
   4 Straight-Grain Kaleidoscope sets per strip set

6¾" Straight-Grain Kaleidoscope

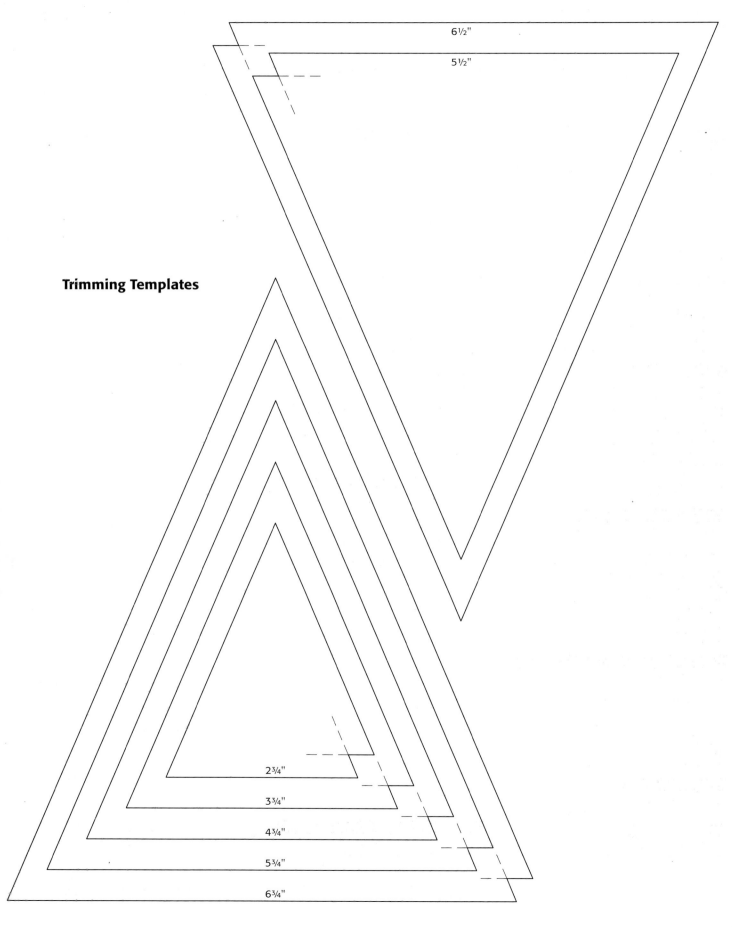

Trimming Templates

6½"

5½"

2¾"

3¾"

4¾"

5¾"

6¾"